CW00740533

Land

CROATIA

a countryside guide
Fourth edition

Sandra Bardwell

SUNFLOWER BOOKS

Fourth edition © 2020
Sunflower Books
PO Box 36160
London SW7 3WS, UK
www.sunflowerbooks.co.uk

All rights reserved.
No part of this
publication may be
reproduced, stored in a
retrieval system, or
transmitted by any form
or by any means,
electronic, mechanical,
photocopying, recording
or otherwise, without
the prior written
permission of the
publishers.

Sunflower Books and
'Landscapes' are Registered
Trademarks.

ISBN 978-1-85691-531-1

Seen on Walk 9 near Podrace

Important note to the reader

We have tried to ensure that the descriptions and maps in this book are error-free at press date. The book will be updated in any future editions. It will be very helpful for us to receive your comments (sent to info@ sunflowerbooks.co.uk, please) for the updating of future editions.

We also rely on those who use this book — especially walkers — to take along a good supply of common sense when they explore. Conditions can change fairly rapidly on the mainland and the islands, and *storm damage or bulldozing may make a route unsafe at any time*. If the route is not as we outline it here, and your way ahead is not secure, return to the point of departure. *Never attempt to complete a tour or walk under hazardous conditions!* Please read carefully the notes on pages 45 to 52, as well as the introductory comments at the beginning of each tour and walk (regarding road conditions, equipment, grade, distances and time, etc). Explore *safely*, while at the same time respecting the beauty of the countryside.

Cover photograph: waterfall at Plitvice Lakes (Walk 18)
Title page: Cistus *(rock roses, Walk 4)*

Photographs: the author, with the exception of pages 6-7, 10, 14-5, 18, 22-3, 36-7, 48, 60-1, 65, 68, 73, 76, 80-1, 86, 89, 93, 95, 97 (top), 114-5, 130, 154, 158-9, 162-3 and the cover: Shutterstock; 21, 26, 54-5, 87, 91, 135, 138-9, 151: istockphoto
Maps: Nick Hill for Sunflower Books. Base map data © OpenStreetMap contributors. Contour data made available under ODbL (opendata commons.org/licenses/odbl/1.0)
A CIP catalogue record for this book is available from the British Library.
Printed and bound in England: Short Run Press, Exeter

● Contents

3

4   Landscapes of Croatia

Preface

From Dubrovnik all the way to the northernmost shores of the Kvarner Gulf, this guide covers 11 of the myriad islands, the Makarska Riviera and two inland areas. It includes Mljet, the Plitvice Lakes, the Krka and Paklenica national parks and Biokovo and Učka nature parks, and it visits or passes eight of Croatia's 10 World Heritage sites. Happily, these bald though impressive facts describe one of the most beautiful and beguiling countries in Europe.

Contrasts and diversity sum up Croatia: tall forests, wind-combed prickly thornbush and juniper on the stony uplands, the miraculous waterfalls in the Plitvice Lakes and Krka national parks, the aridity of the karst landscapes, modern tourist resorts and timeless old villages, the deserted Krajina region and the intensively cultivated Neretva delta, the sociable local ferries and buses.

Each island has a distinct identity, best discovered on foot. Mljet's forests and lakes are unique, and though Koločep, Lopud and Šipan share precious tranquillity, their attractive villages are subtly different. Brač's coastline, punctuated by innumerable coves, is overlooked by the highest peak of the Adriatic islands, while there's more to elongated Hvar than its much-visited capital — old villages, breezy uplands and wide views. On remote Vis, its long and eventful history is very accessible, compact Rab's beaches are without peer. Most of the northern half of Krk is forest-clad, while magnificent rolling uplands, often called moonscapes, characterise the south. Slender Lošinj is dominated by a rugged ridge and is blessed with many delightful coves and inlets, while neighbouring Cres is an island of broad hills, small villages and extensive olive groves. The spectacularly rugged Pelješac peninsula has perhaps the most dramatic mountain scenery of all in a country not short of peaks and high places.

Everywhere the colours of the landscapes are deeper, more vivid and intense than in higher latitudes, particularly the blues and greens of the water — sparkling turquoise, ultramarine and jade green, the deep greens of the forests, the dazzling white of the karst moonscapes, and the vivid pinks and purples of garden plants.

The ever-present sea is a constant source of fascination. It's often calm, painted with mirror-perfect reflections through which fish and aquatic plants are clearly visible. It can also be whipped into turbulent fury by the *bura*, driving blizzards and spiralling vortices of spray across the grey-green water.

Croatia's national and nature parks are the best places to visit for the colourful flora peculiar to limestone country. Still, the parks' special glories are the magnificent forests, especially in Učka, Plitvice Lakes and Paklenica. The light green beeches, venerable wide-spreading oaks, hardy chestnuts, and sombre black pines are all cool havens on hot summer days. The parks are particularly welcoming to walkers, with miles of waymarked and well-maintained paths and trails, some bringing seemingly inaccessible summits within quite easy reach.

Elsewhere, despite the vigorously promoted attractions of the beaches and water sports, walkers certainly aren't ignored, with opportunities for short strolls and full-day excursions. As superbly built old paths and trails between villages, olive groves, vineyards, terraced fields and mountain farms have fallen into disuse, so have many been preserved

for our enjoyment, as have the late 19th-century seashore paths built by Austro-Hungarian benefactors.

From prehistoric times to the end of the 20th century, many empires and events have left their marks on the Croatian landscape. There are prehistoric piles of stones on hilltops, Venetian walls and towers, British and French fortresses, opulent Austro-Hungarian villas, partisans' refuges and poignant memorials commemorating World War II resistance fighters, and even signs of the 1990s strife. Age-old expressions of religious belief survive in innumerable simple, beautiful chapels in small villages. Stone walls and enclosures testify to the centuries-old challenge to wrest a living from the land, even though many are crumbling or are being reclaimed by forests.

Any walk can be enriched by meeting fellow walkers and local people. Croatia draws walkers from many countries near and far, as visitors' books on mountain tops and first-hand experiences testify. Some excursions take you through

Dubrovnik old town

residential areas of everyday Croatia, far removed from nearby resorts. Similarly, using public transport brings you into contact with the patterns of local people's daily lives — workers travelling to the mainland on dawn ferries and people going to town for the early-morning market.

I hope that walking through the countryside rewards you with ever deeper appreciation of the country and its people through an accumulation of small things, from the arduously cultivated fields to ornate villas, gradually revealing how the multifarious cultural influences over the centuries have been absorbed into the landscapes of 21st-century Croatia.

— SANDRA BARDWELL

Acknowledgements

Pat Underwood for the opportunity to explore Croatia and local friends for unflagging support.

Recommended reading

The Rough Guide to Croatia by Jonathan Bousfield. Good background information on the country generally and individual towns and villages. Three of their Snapshot guides are also useful.

Croatia by Anthony Ham and Jessica Lee (Lonely Planet). Unbeatable for invaluable practical information.

Croatia, The Bradt Travel Guide by Piers Letcher and Rudolf Abraham. Easily the most readable of the three with a heartfelt, personal touch.

Useful contacts

For maps, guides, etc

www.amazon.co.uk — for travel guides and phrase books

Stanfords, 7 Mercer Walk, Covent Garden, London WC2H 9FA; tel: 020 7836 1321; www.stanfords.co.uk; e-mail: sales@stanfords.co.uk

The Map Shop, 15 High Street, Upton upon Severn, Worcs WR8 0HJ; tel: 01684 593146 or 0800 085 40 80 (UK only); fax: 01684 594 559; www.themap shop.co.uk; e-mail: themapshop@btinternet.com

For general information and accommodation details

Croatian National Tourist Office, 3rd Floor, 1 Farrier's Yard, 77-85 Fulham Palace Road, London W6 8JA, tel: 0208 5637979, fax: 0208 563 2616; https://croatia.hr/en-GB; e-mail: info@croatia-london.co.uk

www.croatiatraveller.com — an excellent private website with vast amounts of information and good links

www.hicroatia.com — site of the Croatian Camping Union

www.hfhs.hr — Croatian youth hostels

✿ Travel

The quickest and most direct means of travel to Croatia is by **air**. Scheduled flights from Britain land at Zagreb, Split, Pula, Zadar and Dubrovnik; charter airlines link London and UK regional airports with Dubrovnik, Split and Rijeka, while there are budget airline flights to Pula, Rijeka International (on island Krk), Zadar, Split and Dubrovnik. Regular **coach** services link Zagreb and the main coastal towns with other European capitals. Trains operate between Ljubljiana (Slovenia) and Zagreb, and on to Rijeka and Split. Croatia Airlines operates flights between Zagreb and Dubrovnik, Pula, Split, Rijeka and Zadar.

Driving to Croatia from the UK takes at least two days, most directly via Eurotunnel, Brussels, Germany and Austria to Ljubljana, then down to Rijeka. (Citizens of western European countries, Canada and the US do not need a visa.) To use Austrian and Slovenian motorways, you'll need to purchase a *vignette* at the border crossings. Major international and some local hire car companies are widely represented, though car hire is comparatively expensive and fuel costs are on a par with Western Europe. Good car hire deals are available online. **Fly/drive packages** may be a worthwhile means of cutting down costs. Remember that summer traffic is nightmarish and parking an expensive problem almost anywhere. Another possibility is a package holiday at a major resort such as Dubrovnik or Makarska, both good walking centres.

Ferries are part of the experience of travelling in Croatia. Jadrolinija operates the majority of services; off-season timetables are geared to the needs of local people commuting to and shopping on the mainland; additional summer services make it easier to avoid *very* early sailings. Car ferries serve almost all islands; many also enjoy the speed and comfort of hydrofoils and catamarans. Car ferries are expensive, but fares for foot passengers are good value.

Local **buses** meet most ferries and serve outlying towns and villages. The enviable long-distance services operate throughout the Adriatic coast and beyond and are generally frequent, reliable and comparatively inexpensive.

Indeed, such is the extent and frequency of public transport that by astute choice of one, two or even three bases, it's possible to enjoy a car-free holiday.

☀ Car touring

I have outlined nine flexible tours which can be linked in part or whole to suit your own particular interests or time available. The itineraries show how best to use the range of car ferry routes available and are designed to help you plan a holiday of up to a fortnight. The linking thread is the 'Jadranska Magistrala', the coastal Adriatic highway (route 8) between Dubrovnik and Rijeka, from where it is an easy hop to any of the walking bases.

Bridge near Šibenik (Car tour 2, Itinerary 2)

The tours start and finish at places where accommodation is available; other places to stay en route are noted. For detailed information about local sights, track down the official tourist information office (*Turistički Ured;* the staff almost always speak English), as distinct from accommodation agencies which commonly display the 'Information' logo.

Croatia's ever-expanding network of toll motorways is built to high standards — as are all the new main roads everywhere; nevertheless, be prepared for occasional potholes, tight bends, wandering stock and wild boar. Tolls are charged on all Croatian motorways, payable at **toll gates** (see the touring maps); reckon on paying an average of 40kn/100km. For more information go to www.tolls.eu.

Mule and cart-width roads through small towns challenge skill and patience! Many Croatians are given to driving fast and often recklessly, and are fond of driving while using their mobiles; **defensive driving** is recommended. On the islands **petrol stations** are scarce; on the mainland you'll find them on the outskirts of towns. Generally they're open daily, from 7am to 7pm or longer. Contact the Croatian Automobile Association (HAK; tel 1987) in emergencies.

The pullout touring maps are designed to be held out opposite the touring notes and contain all the information you need en route. The map key explains the **symbols** used in the text. (At a larger scale, the Freytag & Berndt 1:200,000 map, 'Croatia Coast Istria — Dubrovnik', is recommended.) The satnav in your car would be most useful in town centres.

In built-up areas the **speed limit** is 50km/h, outside built-up areas 90km/h, on major roads 110km/h (100kph through tunnels), on motorways 130km/h. However, your average touring speed is likely to about 55km/h. Main roads bypass the centre of towns (where parking is almost impossible); should you wish to stop, park as indicated in the notes! Routes to and from car ferry terminals are always clearly signposted.

You'll always find a café or restaurant on or very close to the main roads; shopping for a picnic may be less convenient, so set out with all you'll need.

Please keep in mind the Country code on page 49.

Car tour 1: DUBROVNIK AND BEYOND

Four itineraries, covering Mljet island, the Pelješac peninsula and the coastal route from Dubrovnik to Split

En route: Picnics 1-9, Walks 1-11

Dubrovnik's restored old town *is* Croatia for many travellers and undoubtedly worth a lingering visit. It is also the base for exploring the nearby island of Lokrum and the three Elaphiti islands, Koločep, Lopud and Šipan, which are served only by passenger ferries, and the port of departure for car ferries to the island of Mljet (Itinerary 1).

To reach the town of Orebić on the Pelješac peninsula, the next mainland walking base in this tour, you *can* take a ferry direct from Mljet to Prapratno. But Itinerary 2 describes the route via the 'Jadranska Magistrala' (the coastal highway or E65) — as scenic a drive as you'd wish, winding along the steeply sloping coastal fringe. The road across the Pelješac peninsula is one of the outstanding highlights of travelling through southern Croatia, awesomely scenic. From Orebić I propose six choices for your onward journey.

Itinerary 1: Mljet

33km/20.5mi, 45min driving (to Polače); 38km/23.5mi, 50min driving (to Pomena)
En route: Picnic 6; Walks 4-6
Access: 🚢 to Mljet

From the **Sobra ferry terminal** (🚢) there's a two-way road for about 2.5km; turn right at a junction into **Sobra** (*i* 🏨🏠✕🚌) and there along the waterfront. Continue up to a good two-way road.

At the following junctions, continue towards GOVEÐARI and/or POLAČE (the signs vary); there are no scenic lookouts or lay-bys where you can safely pull off. The main road bypasses the main town of **Babino Polje** (🛉🏨🏠△✕🚌, where there are many old houses and churches dating from the 9th century and later). It leads on, past the entrance to the **Mljet National Park** (Picnic 6; Walks 4-6; map pages 62-63), to **Polače** (*i*🏨🏠✕🚌🚗🚌). About 1km beyond the village ignore the junction on the left for Goveđari

(though it is quite an attractive village; 🛉), and continue to **Pomena** (*i*🏨🏠✕🚌).

The most convenient route to the Pelješac peninsula is the Jadrolinija ferry from Sobra to Prapratno on the south coast of the peninsula (see Transport page 164); from the port it's 3km to the main road; Orebić is 53km further on.

Itinerary 2: Dubrovnik • E65 • Zaton Doli • Ston • Orebić

118km/70.8mi; 2h15min driving
En route: Picnics 1-5; Walks 1-3 (reached from Dubrovnik); Picnic 7, Walk 7 (from Orebić)

From your accommodation in **Dubrovnik★** (*i*🛉👁ffM🏨🏠✕🚌🚇⊕🚢🚌) reach the coastal highway by following signs to SPLIT. The highway is carried across the Rijeka River on the elegant suspension bridge named after Croatia's highly controversial first President, Franjo Tuđjman; there's parking at the far end for one last view of Dubrovnik.

The arboretum at **Trsteno★** (24km ✦△🛢🚌), dating from the 15th century, is definitely worth a visit; otherwise, apart from a few lookouts beside the highway (🎦 at 27km, 34km, 47km and more), there's little to detain you all the way to the Pelješac peninsula junction at **Zaton Doli** (59km; 🚌 300m further on), where you turn left. There are wild boar warning signs ahead!

Only a short distance along, shellfish (especially mussels) may be on sale at a roadside stall. Indeed, if you enjoy shellfish, it's worth diverging to **Mali Ston**, renowned for its seafood restaurants and local wine★ (64km *i*✝🏔🛢🗙🍴). Nearby **Ston★** (65km *i*✝🛢🏛🛢🗙△🍴🛢) is surrounded by a fortified wall more than 5km long and with 20 of the original 40 towers still standing. Dating from the 14th century, it was built mainly to protect the lucrative salt pans. You can walk along the top of the wall (see photo overleaf) by paying a fee at Mali Ston or Ston. There is a large car park in the town centre. For dining with a magnificent view, the Restaurant Bella Vista, just past the Prapatno turn-off, is well named (68km).

Through more vineyards with spectacular views down the north-east coast you come to the seaside village of **Drače** (91km 🗙🚌). Then, in the village of **Janjina** (93km), you'll probably find local wine for sale. The road swings across to overlook the west coast and more dramatic scenery. Past the turn-off to Trstenik (97km 🛢🗙🚌) there's an impressive drive up the side of a steep valley, leading back into vineyard country, past a large World War II resistance monument on the crest close to the

village of **Pijavičino** (103km). Near **Potomje** (105km 🚌) the Dinjač winery offers a temptation, then there's another winery at **Prizdrina** (108km).

Just past the turn-off to Trpanj (110.5km *i*🏔🛢🗙🚌🛢) you start the awesome descent to the coast, including two steepish sections, to **Orebić★** (118km *i*✝🏛M🏔🛢△🗙🚌⊕🚌🛢; Picnic 7; Walk 7).

From Orebić you have five choices for the onward journey (see also Transport page 164):

1) return direct to Dubrovnik;

2) return to the A8 at Zaton Doli and continue north and west along it to Split, via Makarska (*163km/ 101mi; 2h45min driving:* see Itineraries 3 and 4);

3) 🛢 from Trpanj (*i*🏔🛢🗙🛢) on the peninsula's north coast to Ploče (*i*🚌🚌🛢) on the mainland, 43km southeast of Makarska via the A8. The turn-off is 13km from Orebić, and the port 9km further on;

4) cross to Korčula (*i*✝🛢🏛🏔🛢🗙🚌M⊕🚌🛢) and drive to Vela Luka (*i*🛢🗙🚌🚌) at the western end of the island (48km) for a 🛢 to Split;

5) cross to Korčula town for the Dubrovnik/Rijeka 🛢.

Itinerary 3: Zaton Doli • Neum • Ploče • Drvenik • Makarska
104km/62.4mi; 1h30min driving
En route: Picnics 8, 9; Walks 8, 10, 11

This is a varied and interesting drive — through a narrow strip of Bosnia and Herzegovina (its only access to the sea and for which you need just your passport), the rich agricultural lands around the River Neretva, past industrial Ploče, the ferry port of Drvenik and on to the Makarska Riviera.

Heading west from **Zaton Doli**, the first presentation of passports is at a gate on the northwestern side of Uvala Bistrina (6km ). The highway passes through **Neum** (18km), a large town blighted by concrete hotels. The second passport presentation is at the northwestern border (23km). To bypass the two Bosnia and Herzegovina border crossings, a bridge linking Drače on the Pelješac peninsula to the A8 coastal highway at Duboka (between Neum and Opuzen) is scheduled for completion by July 2021. Access roads at both ends will follow eventually. Meanwhile, the existing road through Ston will not be affected.

The highway swings inland to skirt the vast delta of the **River Neretva**, covered with fruit and vegetable plots and where citrus fruits are a specialty. Pass a minor road to the left, to Mala Neretva (38km). Continue through the junction of the road to Mostar (39km). The highway then closely parallels the River Neretva for about 8km; along here look out for roadside fruit stalls. **Ploče** (54km), an industrial and commercial centre, has little to offer other than the terminal for the ferry serving

Trpanj on the Pelješac peninsula.

Where the highway returns to the coast northeast of Ploče, there's a magnificent view, especially of the Pelješac peninsula and Svete Ilija (Walk 7), from a roadside lay-by (61km 📷). Overlooking the headland of Rt Kokuljica a large sign welcomes visitors to the '**Makarska Riviera-Gradac**' at a scenic lookout with seats (63km 📷). The village of **Zaostrog** (72km ⛪🚐M🏖️⛺🗙🚤) could be worth a stop — and there's a nice beach at Gornja Vala, just south of **Drvenik** (76km *i* 🏖️🗙🚤🚌🛥️), the port for the car ferry to Hvar. Beyond

Podgora (🏖️🏠🗙) just below the road, the various seaside towns virtually merge into one all the way to **Makarska**★ (104km *i*⛪M🏖️🏠⛺🗙🚤🏤⊕🛥️🚌; Picnics 8 and 9; Walks 8, 10, 11). Although the highway bypasses the centre of the town, the access road is clearly signed.

Itinerary 4: Makarska • Omiš • Split*

65km/39mi; 1h driving
En route: Picnics 8, 9; Walks 8-11

The first part of the drive from **Makarska** via **Baška Voda** (Walks 8 and 9) to the large town of Omiš is very scenic, especially around Uvala Vrujla, where there's a fine lookout (19km 📷) and another approaching the Marušici turn-off (25km 📷). **Omiš** (39km *i*⛪⛪ 🏖️🏠🗙🚤🚐🚌) is dramatically located near the mouth of the southern side of the River Cetina just downstream from its rugged gorge. Car parks are on the seaward side of the road, before and beyond the sea front.

The rest of the way is through an almost continuous succession of unattractive towns to suburban and downtown **Split**★ (65km *i*⛪ 🚢⛪M🏖️🏠🗙🚤🏤⊕🛥️🚌), which is always busy and congested. The route to the ferry port is well signposted from the highway.

*Consider taking the car ferry from Makarska to Sumartin on the eastern tip of Brač (see Transport, page 164): drive across the island (Car tour 3) to Supetar, then board one of the frequent car ferries to Split. This takes longer than the coast road but is far more enjoyable.

Ston's fortified walls and the salt pans (Itinerary 2)

Car tour 2: CENTRAL DALMATIA

Two itineraries, covering the Makarska Riviera and providing links to Brač, Hvar, Vis and Car tour 6

En route: Picnics 8, 9 and 18, Walks 8-11

Central Dalmatia is a microcosm of Croatia, with a splendidly rugged mountain range overlooking the scenic coast, and a cluster of beautiful islands within easy reach. The city of Split (Croatia's second largest) is the hub for these itineraries, being quite well served by international and national flights, with excellent connections to wide-ranging bus services, and a busy ferry port. Diocletian's Palace, within easy reach of the ferry terminal (and one of Croatia's seven Unesco World Heritage Sites) is reason enough to visit the city, even though you may feel (as I did) that its integrity is perilously threatened by rampant commercialisation.

Itinerary 1 (which can easily be linked with Car tour 1) covers the Makarska Riviera, with walks and picnics in the Biokovo Nature Park. It is also designed to tie in with the tours of Brač, Hvar and Vis (Car tours 3-5). Itinerary 2 offers a good link to Car tour 6.

Itinerary 1: Split • Omiš • Makarska

65km/39mi; 45min driving
En route: Picnics 8, 9; Walks 8-11

An alternative (and in my view, preferable) way to travel from Split to Makarska is to take the ferry from Split to Supetar on Brač (see Car tour 3) and drive across the island to Sumartin on its eastern tip, from where it's a short ferry trip to Makarska (see Transport, page 164). If you're driving the A8 from **Split** to Omiš, the highway initially passes through an almost unbroken succession of suburbs and unattractive towns.

Omiš (26km *i*✝**⊓M**⌂▲✕◻⊠ 🚌) is dramatically located on the southern side of the River Cetina just downstream from its rugged gorge. South from there the highway clings to the coast and the route is very scenic; there is a fine viewpoint 200m south of the Marušici/Lokva turn-off (40km 📷) and another approaching the apex of the bend around Uvala

Vrujla (46km 📷). Pass the turn-off to Baška Voda (58km; Walks 8 and 9) and, 300m beyond a road to Promajna (61km), a picnic area on the right (🍴).

The highway bypasses the centre of **Makarska**★, but the turn-off is well signposted (65km *i*✝M⌂▲△✕◻⊠⊕🚐🚌; Picnics 8 and 9; Walks 8, 10, 11).

Itinerary 2: Split • Trogir • Šibenik • Krka National Park • Zadar

175km/105mi; 2h driving
En route: Picnic 18

This itinerary is proposed as a link with Car tour 6. Highlights of this drive are the walled island town of Trogir and Krka National Park, on what would otherwise be a less than memorable route.

A short stretch of dual carriageway bypasses central Split and is well signposted; ŠIBENIK and TROGIR are the most relevant signs to follow. Turn off left for **Trogir**★ (20km *i*✝**⛴⊓M**⌂▲✕◻⊠), 3km

Split harbour, evening

from the highway; there are several car parks not far from the footbridge to the tiny island on which Trogir sits. A Unesco World Heritage Site, Trogir is a powerful magnet as a superbly preserved medieval town, though even at 9am it can be very crowded.

Return to the highway by the same road to avoid the congested coast road further on. You continue through varied coastal and inland scenery with views of the islands strewn across inshore waters. The small old town of **Primošten** (53km *i✝🏔▲🏕✕🏖*🚐) is worth a diversion; to reach it turn right, then back under the highway.

Via a tunnel you reach **Šibenik** harbour (74km *i✝🏩🛤M🏔▲✕🏖*🚉⊕🚂🚐) and a large car park. The magnificent 16th-century Cathedral of St James (another World Heritage Site) is undoubtedly worth visiting.* To bypass the town, follow signs for ZADAR.

The turn-off on the right for **Krka National Park** is clearly signposted (route 56, 78.5km). Follow this road north, passing

---

*To visit the town, turn-off the highway for Šibenik CENTAR, then turn right at a crossroads and take the next left turn, along Ulica Stjepana Radica. After 1.7km turn left on Ulica Valdimira Nazora and follow this round to the shore; after 450m there's a car park on the right.

over the A1/E6 motorway, to a junction (88.5km) and turn left. Ignore the road entering the park from **Lozovac** (89km) and continue down around some tight bends to the bridge across the Krka River (96km). The small town of **Skradin**, whence the national park ferries depart, is 1km further to the left (97km *i🏔▲✕🏖*🚤). There are large, free car parks in the town centre. For notes about the park, and a short walk suggestion, see Picnic 18 on pages 39-40.

To return, go back to the main road, turn right, cross the motorway and continue towards Šibenik. Turn right towards Vodice to cross the Krka River, where there is a picnic area on the southern side of the bridge (115km 🏕). The highway winds on through lightly wooded plains and hilly country. You pass a huge marina at **Vodice** (121km *i✝🏔▲🏕✕🏖*🚐) and enjoy good island views from **Drage** (144km 🚐).

At Zadar★ (175km *i✝🏩M🏔▲✕🏖*🚉⊕🚤🚐) there's much of interest, notably the old walled town. It's best to park near the bus and train stations: turn left at a major intersection where the highway continues to the right; the stations are 1km further on the left — and it's just a little over 1km (15 minutes) to walk to the town centre.

Car tour 3: BRAČ

Two itineraries, the first taking in the summit of Vidova Gora and the monastery of Blaca, the second the scenic north coast

En route: Picnic 10; Walks 12-14

Brač is distinguished as the location of Vidova Gora (778m), the highest peak in the Adriatic islands, as well as the extraordinary Blaca Monastery and famous Zlatni Rat beach. Its indented, low-profile north coast contrasts sharply with the mountainous southern half of the island. Brač is blessed with a good road network and some fine waymarked walking routes.

The highlights of this tour are the summit of Vidova Gora and the remote monastery of Blaca (Itinerary 1). But rather than returning direct to Bol afterwards, I highly recommend Itinerary 2: drive via Škrip, the oldest settlement on Brač, Splitska and the island's scenic north coast. There are no specific picnics or short walks here, but the villages en route offer ample opportunities for picnicking or more formal dining. Generally, the roads are narrow and tortuous, and opportunities for stopping very few.

Both itineraries *could* be covered in a full day, but there's much to be said for spreading them over two days.

Access to Brač

There are two options (see Transport on page 164). Either take the ferry from Makarska to Sumartin or the one from Split to Supetar. From the ferry landing at **Sumartin** (🕆🛏🔺🔺✕🚤) the road passes the village of **Selca**

(*i*♿⛰⛰✕🚐) to the hamlet of
Gornje Humac (16km ⛰🚐),
where you turn left for the
dramatic, steep descent to **Bol**
(27km/16.2mi).

The road from the ferry
terminal at **Supetar** (*i*♿⛰⛰⛰△✕
🚌🚭⊕🚤🚐) leads southeast
around the edge of the town to a
roundabout; continue to the right
for BOL, then go left at the next
junction. From here it's a straightforward drive across the island via
Gornje Humac down to **Bol**
(35km/21mi).

Itinerary 1: Bol • Gornje Humac • Pražnice • Stup • Vidova Gora • Blaca Monastery • Stup • Gornje Humac • Bol

59km/35.4mi, 1h driving
En route Picnic 10, Walks 12-14
From **Bol**★ (*i*♿⛰M⛰⛰△✕🚌🚭
⊕🚤🚐) drive up to **Gornje
Humac** (10km ⛰🚐), turn left to
the hamlet of **Pražnice** (14km)
and left again towards NEREŽIŠĆA.
Leave the main road at a place
called **Stup**, at a junction signposted to VIDOVA GORA and
PUSTINJE BLACA (23.5km). At a
sharp left bend (24.1km) an
unsurfaced road to the right is
signposted to PUSTINJE BLACA.
Turn right here, and pick up the
notes for Alternative walk 14
on page 94 to visit **Blaca
Monastery** (photo page 93).

Continue along the surfaced
road, mostly single track, through
pine woodland among scattered
limestone outcrops. *Watch out* for
wandering sheep, especially lambs
in late April. Where the road bends
right through a gateway (29.5km),
park in the small car park on the

right and walk on to the summit of
Vidova Gora, shown on page 91
(Picnic 10, Walk 13).

Return to the main road
(35.5km) then return to **Bol** direct
or turn left for Itinerary 2.

Itinerary 2: Stup • Škrip • (Supetar) • Splitska • Postira • Pučišća • Pražnice • Gornje Humac • Bol

84.8km/50.9mi, 1h30min driving
From **Stup** continue northwest,
soon descending to a junction
(39.3km) where you turn right*
along a narrow twisting road to
Škrip★ (43.2km ♿M⛰✕🚌), the
island's oldest settlement. The
Museum of Brač is on the right.

From here continue to the
north coast road, meeting it above
the small town of **Splitska**
(45.8km ⛰✕🚌🚐). Both Splitska
and **Postira** (49.8km *i*⛰⛰✕🚌
🚐) are below the main road; the
latter is the more attractive. After
more twists and turns, ups and
downs, it's well worth detouring
down into **Pučišća** (63.8km
i⛰⛰✕🚌🚐), at the end of a
deep inlet. This is the centre of
marble production on the island.
From there the road stays true to
form for the climb to **Pražnice**
(70.8km), from where it's plain
sailing back to **Bol** (84.8km).

---

*Or continue via Supetar (adding
6km and missing out Škrip): stay on
the main road, past junctions on the
left to Nerežišća then Ložišće. Continue over the ridge and down to the
outskirts of **Supetar**, past a road to
Milna on the left and on to a roundabout. Here turn left for the town
(parking is on the left 1km along).

Left: Škrip chapels (Itinerary 2)

Just one itinerary, concentrating on timeless villages and panoramic views

En route: Picnics 11-13; Walks 15-17

Hvar is a long lizard of an island dominated by the high precipitous ridge that forms its spine. Hvar town is immensely popular, and with good reason. As a convenient walking base there is little to choose between Hvar town and Stari Grad, although the latter is definitely quieter.

This short, very scenic tour takes you across the plateau at the western end of the island, past small villages where little seems to have changed for a long time, and extensive areas of terraced hillsides; there's a small, superbly located restaurant near the highest point. The preferred direction is clockwise, the better to appreciate the wide views. The road is nominally two lanes wide, though it's a tight squeeze in several places. Beware — buses ply this road!

Access to Hvar

There are two options (see Transport, page 164). Either take the ferry from Split to **Stari Grad** and drive to **Hvar town** (19km) or take the ferry from Drvenik to **Sućuraj** (*i* 🕇 🍴 ⛰ ⛵ △ ✕ ⊕ 🚤), from where it's a straightforward drive via **Jelsa** (*i* ⛰ ⛰ △ ✕ 🅿 🚤 🚌) to **Stari Grad** (59km) and on to **Hvar town** (78km/47mi).

Itinerary: Hvar town • Stari Grad • Selca • Brusje • Hvar town

42km/25.2mi; 1h30min driving

From **Hvar town**★ (*i* 🕇 🍴 🏛 M ⛰ ⛰ ✕ 🅿 ⊕ 🚤 🚌; Picnics 11, 12; Walk 16) take the modern road to Stari Grad. It's a long climb (with no scenic viewpoints) to the 1.5km-long tunnel and a fairly steep descent to the **Stari Grad ferry terminal** (✕ 🅿 🚤 and shop).

Continue from there for 2km, turn left, then then take the first left and the first right, to reach a car park (beside the bus stop). From here it's only a short walk to the centre of **Stari Grad** and the harbour★ shown on page 95

(19km *i* 🕇 M ⛰ ⛰ ⛰ ✕ 🅿 🚤 🚌; Picnic 13; Walks 15 and 17).

Return to a junction on the left (22km); not far beyond a quarry on a U-bend (23.4km) is the only steep climb on the road (10%). The not unattractive hamlet of **Selca** (25km) seems to be on its last legs; there's a good view westwards to Brač's indented coast and the village of Murvica from here. Selca's chapel and burial ground is on the right (25.5km); there's an informal car park on the left with good view of the hamlet and of Bol on Brač (📷).

The road leads on past extensive sheer cliffs and passes over the tunnel entrance on the main road, where there's a slightly alarming steep drop off the right-hand edge of the road (26.6km). Then you continue through the characteristic landscape of terraces and stone walls, most dating from the 19th century, originally for vine cultivation, later for lavender.

At a junction (27.8km), where a track leads to Svete Nikola (Walk 17, photo pages 102-103) there's an informal car park with picnic

Hvar town from Španjola fort (Picnic 12)

tables and fine local views. Nearby is a limekiln, built in 1914 but never used, and a large, informative map. It's only a short distance to the crest (28.3km ✕🖼) and Vidikovac Levanda, a restaurant specialising in lamb on the spit and with views in both directions, including the Pakleni Islands and the island of Vis beyond. About 300m further on there's a pull-off on the left for a good view of the hamlet of Velo Grablje below. Then you'll find an informal car park (also the bus stop once weekly) opposite the unsignposted turn-off to the village of **Velo Grablje** (30km). You could of course drive down to the hamlet, but parking space there is not guaranteed. Walk 16 is a linear route from Velo Grablje to Hvar town.

Further on, at the start of a U-bend, a lay-by on the right with a cross and an oratory (30.8km 🖼), affords an excellent view of Selca, Stari Grad, the summit of Svete Nikola, and a stone shelter on the slope below to the left. Then, at the start of a wide right bend, it's possible to pull off on the left, beside a tall cypress, for a fine view over the countryside and across the northern end of Brač to the island of Šolta (33.2km 🖼).

In the village of **Brusje** (35.5km), just past a minor road on the left and near where several cars might be parked in or near the centre of the village, is a 1941-1945 war memorial, complete with the hammer and sickle insignia.

Soon the road starts to descend through a narrow valley and with less than 1km to go, the newer residential areas of **Hvar town** suddenly appear ahead. At a T-junction (41km) turn left to the car park beside the nearby bus station.

Car tour 5: VIS

Two itineraries, taking in historic caves, vineyards and coastal villages, the second one a slightly longer route via the southeastern corner of the island

En route: Picnics 14-17

The farthest flung and smallest of the central Dalmatia islands featured in this guide, Vis also conveys the keenest sense of remoteness. The forested massif of Mount Hum dominates the southern half of the island, and the two main towns, Vis and Komiža, are crowded around bays on the north and southwest coasts. Two long inland valleys are intensively cultivated, mainly with vineyards. It's worth noting that you can hire a car, scooter or cycle in Vis town.

The tour takes you to the attractive small town of Komiža, then two caves high on the slopes of Mount Hum which briefly served as the headquarters of Tito's Partisans during 1944 (see Josip Broz Tito, page 70), through a vineyard-covered valley, and back to Vis town either directly (Itinerary 1) or via the southeast coast (Itinerary 2).

Access to Vis
Ferry and catamaran services from Split to Vis town.

Itinerary 1: Vis town • Komiža • Podšpilje • Titova Špilja • Svete Duh • Podšpilje • Vis town
37.4km/22.4mi; 1h driving
En route: Picnics 14-17

From **Vis town** ★ (*i* ✝ ⛪ 🚌 M ⛰ ⛺ ✕ 🚗 🅿 ⊕ ⛴ 🚐; Picnics 14, 15) join the main road leading west. Pass a turn-off on the left signed to Podselje and continue up the long valley, extensively planted with vineyards. The steep climb (10%) starts at the 4km mark, up past an eye-catching rounded white church on the left, Gospa od Plantice (11th century), and on to the pass (at 330m). There's a parking area on the right, perfect for the spectacular view of Komiža and its bay. To have a closer look at the small 12th-century church of Svete Mihovil nearby, go up a short flight of steps on the south side of the road.

A series of skilfully designed bends wind down the precipitous mountainside, dense with old terraces. At a junction where Podšpilje is to the left, bear right towards KOMIŽA (*do not* continue straight on, as the road ahead leads to a maze of narrow lanes and minimal chance of parking). Take the second left and, just past a playing field, parking is available on the right (10.7km). Walk down to **Komiža** harbour from here (*i* ✝ 🚌 ⛰ ⛺ ✕ ⊕ 🚐).

To continue, return to the Podšpilje junction and turn right, up past prominent Svete Nikola Benedictine monastery (see left). The road winds up, over a high point (Vrh Iznad Podhumja, 285m). Continue down through the hamlet of **Podhumlje** to **Podšpilje** (19.4km; shop). Turn left here at the junction signposted towards ZENA GLAVA. Further on, at another junction (20km), bear left. Continue straight on where a minor road leads left to the handful of houses called Borovik. Drive up the partly cultivated valley to a sharp left bend (21.4km) and small parking area for Tito's caves (**Titova Špilja**; Picnic 16, photograph overleaf).

Continue steeply up the road; on a left bend, from where a lookout tower on Hum summit is in sight, park on the verge where a gravel track leads to right to the small chapel of **Svete Duh**

*Svete Nikola overlooking **Komiža***

view back down the long wide valley. Although VIS is signposted left here, down the main road, turn *right* along the minor road, for more opportunities to overlook Vis town. Continue north to a junction (34.1km 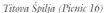) and turn left. There are viewpoints ( ) at the second and third U-bends. Follow the road west to the main road; turn right and it's only 200m to **Vis harbour** (37.4km).

Itinerary 2: Podstražje • Rukavac • Milna • Vis town
adds 14.6km/9mi; 15min driving
Turn right at the junction outside **Plisko Polje**. This narrow, mostly single-track road that leads south and southeast to the hamlet of **Podstražje** (33.7km ✕ in season; shop), just before which is a good view down to Uvala Rukavac and Ravnik island. From here turn right, down towards RUKAVAC and SREBRENA ( ). Continue fairly steeply down to the tranquil small harbour and the end of the road at **Rukavac** (35.2km ✕ in season;). There's some scope for picnics on the flat rocky shore, but no shade.

Return to the junction at **Podstražje** (36.7km) and turn right to **Milna** (38.9km). There's a beach here, but in spring it unfortunately collects both seaweed and a rich variety of flotsam. The road improves from here and leads northeast past **Zenka**, around a sharp bend (40.7km), then generally west, through vineyards, to a T-junction (44km). Turn left here and drive up the narrow winding road to a junction (45.8km). Join the signposted main road and turn right, down to **Vis town** (52km).

(22.4km ; Picnic 17). Access to Hum (587m), the highest point on the island, is prohibited — there's a barrier across the road, the military lookout tower is manned and there's a sign prohibiting photography.

So return to the main road at **Podšpilje** (25.4km) and turn left. A few hundred metres along, wine and liqueurs may be on sale at an attractive house on the left. The road leads northeast through the valley dense with small vineyards; in the hamlet of **Plisko Polje** (29.4km ✕) you may also find a cellar door wine outlet. Continue along the narrow road (*beware* of the sharp unprotected drop on the right), to a junction on the right (31.2km).

Here you have a choice. For a slightly longer itinerary taking in the southeastern corner of the island, see Itinerary 2 below.

Itinerary 1 continues to Vis town. Drive straight on up the winding road to a junction on the crest (32.9km) with a tall cross and a memorial to RAF men lost over Croatia during World War II. It's worth pausing here for the

Car tour 6: LAKES, WATERFALLS, CANYONS

Two itineraries, one visiting the Plitvice Lakes and Paklenica national parks, the second taking you on to Rijeka for a link to Car tour 7

En route: Picnics 19-22; Walks 18-21

Plitvice Lakes National Park should be among the most memorable experiences of a holiday in Croatia. It is possible to visit the park on a long day out from Zadar, but this would be too much like a marathon; fortunately there's plenty of accommodation near the lakes. The route outlined here follows scenic motorways and good major roads.

Itinerary 1 takes you to and from Plitvice and on to Paklenica National Park. The greater part of the route passes through the territory of the ill-fated Serbian Republic of Krajina, established by Serbian forces in 1991 during the Homeland War. It extended north and northwest from the town of Knin, through the Plitvice Lakes area, to less than 50km from Zagreb. Croatians were driven from their homes and many chose not to return after the Republic collapsed in 1995. However, the region is enjoying a renaissance with new and restored buildings much in evidence, and more facilities for visitors and locals alike.

Itinerary 1: Zadar • Obravac • Zaton • Gračac • Bruvno • Korenica • Plitvice Lakes National Park • Gracac • Zaton • Maslenika • Starigrad-Paklenica

313km/195mi; 5h45min driving
En route: Picnics 19-22; Walks 18-21

Leave **Zadar★** (*i* ♦ ⛽ 🚉 M ♠ ▲ ✕ 🍴 ♇ ⊕ 🚃 🚐) on route 8 from a large intersection on the northeastern side of the city. Follow the divided highway northeast to join the A1/E65 motorway. At the **Maslenica interchange** (32km), switch to the E71 which winds up impressively into the Velebit foothills. There's a large car park at **Marune** (50km), just before the 6km-long **Sveti Rok tunnel**. Continue on the far side to the **Gornja Ploče interchange** (70km), signposted to PLITVICE LAKES along route 522.

Continue through the vast wide

Večko Kula (Picnic 21 from Starigrad-Paklenica)

valley of cultivated fields and woodlands, with occasional roadside stalls selling local cheese and honey, to the small town of **Korenica** (110km ♠ ✕ 🍴 ♇ 🚐). From a junction at **Borje** (113km *i* △ ✕ 🍴 🚐) the road winds on through forested country to the

25

Plitvice Lakes National Park★ (128km *i*🏠🏠🏠🗙🚏🚐; Picnic 19; Walk 18), shown overleaf, on pages 105-107 and the cover.

Return to the **Maslenica** motorway interchange, and follow route 8 to **Paklenica National Park** and **Starigrad-Paklenica★** (272km *i*🛉🍽🏠🏠🛆🗙🚏🚐⊕🚐; Picnics 20-22; Walks 19-21; photos pages 108, 110, 113).

Itinerary 2: Starigrad-Paklenica to Rijeka

170km/102mi; 2h30min driving

This route linking Car tours 6 and 7 is undoubtedly a scenic drive, but in places the highway is extremely tortuous, even by local standards; *safe overtaking places are rare*. The road surface is generally very good; there are a few signposted car parks on the seaward side of the road and several unannounced lay-bys.

From **Starigrad-Paklenica**, as the road winds around innumerable small inlets, the views across the channel are dominated by the starkly white, rocky islands of Pag and Goli Otok. Pag is an extraordinary sight: its seemingly endless, almost monochrome north coast topped by wind turbines. The view on a sunny day is of three bands of sharply defined colours: sky blue, white and deep blue.

Karlobag (37km *i*🏠🏠🏠🗙🚏🚏🚐) is the first settlement of any size; there's a pay car park on the seaward side. The turn-off to **Jablanac/Stinica** for the Rab car ferry is signposted (64km 🚢). (Rab makes an excellent stepping stone between Zadar and Rijeka, via Krk, linked by a bridge to the mainland — something to keep in mind for another day.)

Then you come to a high, tortuous inland stretch, across the slopes of the mountains in North Velebit National Park, en route to **Senj** (102km *i*🛉M🏠🏠🏠🗙🚏🚏🚐). The pay car park is by the harbour; the town is notorious for being in the firing line of destructive *bura* winds (see page 47). The Split/Zagreb motorway is accessible from the southern end of the large town.

Further on it's worth stopping in **Novi Vinodolski** (124km 🏠🏠🏠🗙🚏🚏🖼) for views back to the Velebit mountains, if nothing else; there's a pay car park at the harbour. Around **Crikvenica** (132km) there's a marked change: busier traffic, industrial complexes, and a spectacular view of Krk bridge. The turn-off for the bridge to that island (148km) is on the right-hand side of the road (see Car Tour 7). From here to Rijeka the highway passes another access road to the Zagreb–Split motorway (157km), then goes through industrial areas and past the port, to a major junction. Turn right here into **Rijeka★** (170km *i*🛉🛉 M🏠🏠🏠🗙🚏🚏⊕🚐🚐), or continue straight on towards PULA for Opatija and Lovran.

Left: typical boardwalk at Plitvice Lakes (Walk 18, Picnic 19)

Three itineraries, one on the mainland and two on islands. Each itinerary offers fine walking and picnicking suggestions.

En route: Picnics 23, 24; Walks 22-33

This is the most populous region in the Adriatic and probably the most developed for tourism, with an array of car ferry services between the mainland and the islands and between the islands themselves, offering various island-hopping itineraries.

Rijeka is the hub, with good rail and bus connections but limited international and national flights. It's the most industrialised of the coastal cities and towns, but its pedestrianised centre is a pleasant retreat for whiling away the time between ferries. The three itineraries on this tour cover the Lovran-Opatija Riviera, the adjacent Učka Nature Park, and the islands of Krk and Rab, with possibilities for onward travel to two islands which merit separate tours (Lošinj and Cres; see Car tours 8-9).

Itinerary 1: Rijeka • Opatija • Lovran

20.5km/12.3mi, 30min driving
En route: Walks 22-25

From **Rijeka** follow the road towards PULA (route 8). Ignore a turn-off to Opatija (3.5km); continue past the road to Matulji (10.5km; access to Walk 24), then the turn-off to **Volosko** (⏏⛰✕ ▆🚌) and **Opatija★** (11.5km *i✝🚉 ⏏⛰✕▆🚉⊕🚌*; Walk 22). Continue along the narrow winding road (route 66) to **Lovran★** (20.5km *i✝🚉 ⏏⛰✕▆ 🚉⊕🚌*; Walks 23, 25).

Both Lovran and Opatija are well placed as bases for the walks described in this section, Lovran being the quieter of the two towns. Here you can savour the contrasts between the many well-preserved 19th-century Austro-Hungarian villas in the coastal towns, and the superb beech forests and mountain scenery in **Učka Nature Park** overlooking the coast. Walk 24 involves a long but scenic drive into the mountains to the starting point at Poklon.

Just 27km south of Lovran via the very pretty Rijeka–Pula coast road is the 2.6km steep access road to the ferry terminal at Brestova (✕ ⛴), from where you can cross to **Cres/Lošinj** (Car tour 9).

Itinerary 2: Krk by road bridge*

50.3km/31.2mi, just over 1h driving from the mainland to Baška
En route: Picnic 24; Walks 29-33

Some 22km eastwards from Rijeka a road bridge from the coastal highway runs over to Krk. (This bridge is also passed on Car tour 6, Itinerary 2.) The turn-off is sign-posted OTOK KRK; you pass through the toll or 'Peage' (35kn per car, payable also in euros and on arrival only). The main 'Krčki Most' (bridge) is 1.43km long, crossing the tip of the tiny island of **Svete Marko**; there's a car park on the right, about 200m further on.

---

*You can also get to Krk by car ferry from Rab (via Lopar to Valbiska) and from Cres (via Merag to Valbiska); from Valbiska it's 10km to the main road across the island; turn right for Krk town.

Svete Marin, Kaldanac Park (Rab) (Picnic 23)

Four of the five walks on Krk are based at the lovely town of Baška on the south coast (photo pages 138-139), and the fifth starts from Krk town. So there's no need for a 'car tour' as such here, but don't overlook Krk old town (if only to conclude that Baška's old town is more charming and less commercialised). If you plan to walk near Baška, don't miss St Lucy's church in Jurandvor (see Walk 29, page 112 and 'Glagolitic script' page 113).

Continue past the turn-offs to a string of coastal towns (of which **Malinska** is easily the most attractive), past the junction of the road signposted to the CRES/LOŠINJ FERRY at **Valbiska** (23.6km from the highway; ✕🚌🚐). Then comes the turn-off to KRK TOWN (29.3km) — follow signs to CENTAR; there's a car park near the bus station and no more than 10minutes' walk from **Krk old town★** (*i*⛪🏨🎭M ▲▲⌂✕🏪⊕🚐; Walk 33).

Continue on, past the junction for the small town of Punat (34.3km *i* ▲▲⌂△✕🏪🚐). From there the road climbs steeply. Immediately beyond a sign welcoming you to Baška, there's a lookout on the right (39.5km 📷). The road winds down through many bends into a long valley, through the villages of **Draga Bašćanska** (45km ✕🏪🚐), where Walk 30 ends, and **Jurandvor** (47.6km ⛪) to **Baška★** (50.3km *i*⛪🏨🎭M▲▲⌂✕🏪⊕🚐; Picnic 24, Walks 29-32).

Itinerary 3: Rab via Krk

11km/7mi, 15min drive from the ferry terminal at Lopar to Rab town
En route: Picnic 23; Walks 26-28
There is no car ferry service direct from Rijeka to Rab town (only a catamaran). Travelling from Rijeka*, the easiest option is to go via Valbiska on Krk (Itinerary 2 above), then take a ferry to Lopar on Rab. From the terminal at Lopar drive south for 1.3km to a junction on the right, from where it's 10.8km to the turn-off to Rab town centre.

The picnic and walks on Rab are based on **Rab town★** (*i*⛪🏨 M▲▲⌂✕🏪🚐⊕⛱🚐) and **Lopar★** (*i*▲▲⌂△✕🏪🚐⛱🚐), a straightforward, short drive apart, for which reason no specific car tour is described here.

Rab's many beaches and the well-preserved old walled town (photo page 135) are the island's main attractions. A long bare limestone ridge, rising directly from the east coast, shelters most of the western half of the island, making it a luxuriantly wooded oasis.

---

*There are two other approaches: one is from Stinica, off the Jablanac road on the mainland (see Itinerary 2 of Car tour 6): turn-off the E65 coastal highway 104km from Zadar or 107km from Rijeka, down to the port at **Jablanac** (▲▲⌂✕🏪⛴), a further 3km. Take the ferry to Mišnjak, from where it's 9.5km to the turn-off to Rab town centre. The other is by ferry from Merag on Cres, 10.5km from Cres town via a two-way road, to Valbiska, Krk then another ferry to Lopar on Rab

Car tour 8: LOŠINJ

Three itineraries, the first two different approaches to Veli Lošinj, the third the car tour 'proper' (although it's only a 30-minute drive!), taking in the far south of the island.

En route: Picnics 25 and 26; Walks 34-36

Lošinj is separated from Cres by a narrow, bridged channel, overlooked by the wooded Osorščica ridge. This impressive massif tapers southeastwards to the slender southern half of the island, where you'll find the neighbouring towns of Mali Lošinj and Veli Lošinj, the recommended bases for walks on the island.

Access to Lošinj

There are two options, both via Cres: either take the ferry from Valbiska on Krk to Merag and drive from there (see Itinerary 1) or take the ferry from Brestova on the mainland to Porozina and drive from there (Itinerary 2).

Itinerary 1: Merag (Cres) to Veli Lošinj

70km/43.3mi; 1h15min driving
En route: Picnic 26; Walks 34-36

From **Merag** (✵) the road winds steeply up then down to the main road across Cres (10.5km); continue along the narrow road, past the junction for Cres town (13km). Just beyond the junction on the right for Valun and Lubenice (20.5km), it's worth detouring to the left along a minor road via the hamlet of **Orlec** (23.5km ⬛) for fine views eastwards across the islands of Krk and Rab to the mainland.

Turn right to return to the main road (25km) and continue south, past the village of **Belej** (36km ✵) and on down to **Osor**★ (46km *i*⬛M△✵⬛⬛; Walks 34, 35; photos pages 151, 154). The road leads on south along the foot of the wooded Osorščica ridge, past the outskirts of **Nerezine** (50.6km), where Walk 34 begins, and then across the narrowest part of the island to the fringes of **Mali**

Lošinj★ (67km *i*⬛M⬛⬛⬛✵⬛ ⬛⊕⬛⬛). Continue past the Cikat junction (Itinerary 3) to car parks on the edge of the small town of **Veli Lošinj**★ shown on pages 158-159 (70km *i*⬛⬛M⬛ ⬛✵⬛⬛; Picnic 26, Walk 36).

Itinerary 2: Porozina (Cres) to Veli Lošinj

83km/51.5mi; 1h40min driving
En route: Picnic 26, 30; Walks 34-36

From **Porozina** (⬛⬛✵⬛⬛) the road climbs steadily to a scenic lookout (59.1km ⬛; Picnic 30) and on down to the junction with the road from Merag (68.8km), from where you pick up Itinerary 1 above.

Itinerary 3: Veli Lošinj/Mali Lošinj • Grgoščak • Pogled • Mrtvaška • Svete Ivan • Mali Lošinj/Veli Lošinj

17km/10.2mi; a 30min drive from the junction on the main road, 3km from Veli Lošinj and 0.8km from Mali Lošinj
En route: Picnics 25, 26; Walk 36

Apart from the first very few miles, this is a scenic drive *par excellence*, to the southern tip of the island. There's an historic church to visit, a short stroll along the coast, and perhpas a swim at Mrtvaška's shingle cove. *Take a picnic* (no cafés or shops en route; cold drinks may be available at Mrtvaška).

View south from near Sis across Cres (Picnic 30)

At a roundabout turn-off the **Mali Lošinj/Veli Lošinj** road towards CIKAT. Go up past a huge Konzum supermarket; then, at traffic lights, turn left, and keep left at the second junction towards SV IVAN. The road, bitumen all the way, becomes a single-lane road (2.5km) which widens out in places. There are several lay-bys (📷): the first is on the left about 75m along (good view of Mali Lošinj and the Osorščica ridge). You pass a sign to BALVANIDA (5km; Walk 36), then come to the next viewpoint, at **Grgoščak** (5.5km; local coast views). A third lookout is 1km further on, about 50m north of the 241m-high point known as **Pogled** (fine views of the coast, myriad small islands to south and, in the opposite direction, the high, wooded Osorščica ridge).

Before the very steep, winding descent, pull over for the fine vista of Ilovik, the largest of the nearby islands. The road ends a few metres past a sharp left bend, almost at sea level, at **Mrtvaška** (8.5km; Picnic 25). Park on the right (small fee during summer); the lower car park is for subscribers only.

On the way back there's one stop you must make, at **Svete Ivan** (13.7km ✝📷🎐). There are four roadside parking areas up to 150m downhill from the church and another directly below it. Walk back to the waymarked path to the small, plain 18th-century church dedicated to San Giovanni Basta; mass is celebrated here annually on 24 June. A panorama diagram on the wall indicates what you can see from here: Veli Lošinj, Rovinska, mainland mountains and numerous islands. Then continue back to the main road (17km).

Car tour 9: CRES

Two itineraries, both on the northern half of the island
En route: Picnics 27-30; Walk 37

Cres has much more of an old-world feel than does Lošinj; there are still several timeless villages, just managing to survive, and nowhere to match Mali Lošinj as a resort. Two simple itineraries offer a taste of this peace and timelessness.

The first takes in some secluded beaches at Valun and the dramatic clifftop village of Lubenice. The second visits Beli, a tiny hilltop village of 40 souls above the northeast coast — a special place. An ornithological reserve protects the habitat of the endangered Eurasian griffon (and other species), and it's the home of the Caput Insulae Eco-Centre. It houses excellent displays of all aspects of the islands' natural history, especially the Eurasian griffon. There should always be some birds in residence, either temporarily while recuperating after injury, or permanently because they're no longer able to fend for themselves in the wild, because of injury or poisoning.

Access to Cres
Access as Lošinj; see page 30 for two itineraries from the ferries to the base, Cres town.

Itinerary 1: Cres town • Valun • Lubenice • Cres town
36km/21.6mi; 1h driving
En route: Picnics 27-29; Walk 37
This straightforward tour visits two very different villages southwest of Cres town.

From **Cres town** (*i*✝⛪️🍴M⛰️ ⛰️△✕🚆🅿️⊕📷⛴️🚌; Walk 37) drive south along the main road;

turn right (7.5km) along a minor road signed to *VALUN* and *LUBENICE*. Generally two lanes wide, the road descends westwards with three steep (10%) sections and numerous bends, some quite tight. A formal (by local standards) parking area at (9.5km 📷) affords superb views of the west coast of Cres and of Istria. Pass a signposted junction where Lubenice is to the left (12km) and continue down, steeply at first, to car parks on both sides of the road (13km); there is no direct vehicle access to

Lubenice (Picnic 29)

the village of **Valun**★ (*i*✛△**fT**M⌂ ■; Picnic 28).

Valun, at the head of a broad, steep-sided bay and blessed with two fine beaches and some enticing waterside restaurants, plays an important part in helping to preserve the island's Glagolitic heritage (see 'Glagolitic script' page 143).

To continue, drive back up to the Lubenice junction (14km) and turn right along the narrow road; it's single track in places, with a couple of tight bends and one 10% gradient. Around a bend, pull in right (14.2km) to visit the nearby church of **Svete Marko**, once the parish church for the settlement of Bućev, whose inhabitants decided life would be better on the coast and moved down to found Valun. The small church has a simple yet beautiful interior and there's a tablet beside the door in Glagolitic script. Near the entrance gate the grave of scholar Monsor Anton Benvin (1935-1996) also bears a Glagolitic inscription.

No more than 200m further on, continue straight on for Lubenice. Pass through **Podol** (16.2km) —just a few inhabited houses and a small vineyard. If possible, pull off on the right at a sharp left bend (17.6km 🕾) for a view of Vransko Jezero, the island's fresh water storage. Continue up and across the plateau, through a pine plantation and down to the car park at the entrance to **Lubenice**★ (19km ✛⌂▲**fT**✕M■🕾 and cellar door wine sales; Picnic 29).

Lubenice is quite extraordinary, perched on the edge of a 400m-high cliff. Settlement dates back 4000 years, although now there's only a handful of residents, most or all of whom are older than 65, plus several churches, a couple of restaurants, and possibly local honey for sale.

From here return direct to **Cres town** (36km).

Itinerary 2: Cres town • Beli • Cres town

38km/22.8mi; 1h driving
En route Picnic 30; Walk 37

You could visit Beli en route to or from the ferry at Porozina. An Autotrans bus service to Beli departs Cres town at 06.30, returning 13.30 (weekdays only), making bus travel practicable for a short visit; there is some overnight accommodation in the village. Drive northwards from **Cres town** along the road to Merag and Porozina, past the turn-off to Merag (2.5km). At a major junction (12km), turn-off right for BELI. There is plenty of parking on the right at this junction (🕾), where a fine short walk leads to Picnic 30.

The narrow, mostly single track road (with unsigned passing places) winds down to Beli, steeply near the end; the free car park is at the village entrance.

From here you can explore the village of **Beli**★ (19km *i*✝✛**fT**M ⌂△✕■🚍🕾). The Beli Visitor Centre and Rescue Centre for Vultures (open daily except Monday; entry fee) is a must. The exhibitions comprehensively cover local and regional history and the exceptionally rich biodiversity of the region, and you can learn about the resident griffon vultures in the rescue centre and watch them on a large screen. There's also the intricate network of 'Tramuntana' marked walking (and bike) trails, but they're not easy to follow. The quiet old village is also worth exploring. For more information, go to www.beli visitorcentre.eu.

✿ Picnics and short walks

The beaches, secluded coves and inlets, the shady woodlands, the scenic mountaintops of Croatia's Adriatic coast and islands all offer opportunities for outdoor dining. Picnic grounds, with tables and other facilities, are quite common, especially in some national parks, but still be prepared with something to sit on.

All the picnic spots recommended in this section are easy to reach; some follow parts of walks described elsewhere, others are fine short walks in their own right. None is more than 50 minutes from a safe parking place or public transport, the majority are much closer (times shown are out and *back*).

The location of each picnic is shown by the symbol *P* (printed in green) on the relevant walking or touring map, and some are illustrated. The symbol (○) indicates a site in full sun. For transport details by bus or ferry, see pages 133-134. **Please keep in mind the Country Code on page 41.**

Fill your pack with oven-fresh bread, *pršut* (Croatia's gourmet ham), cheese (especially the dry, slightly salty *paški sir* from the island of Pag), locally grown olives, pickled vegetables, fresh lettuce, cucumber, tomatoes, stone fruit or figs from an outdoor market … and a bottle of local wine or beer.

1 Lokrum (map page 56, photographs pages 54-55)
⛴ to Lokrum. 50min on foot. Follow the Short walk on page 54; picnic on the rocks (○) or in shade on the **northern shore** by ❼ or south of ❽, or have lunch at the secluded restaurant in the former monastery.
A short ferry trip from busy Dubrovnik to the peace of historic Lokrum, a special forest reserve.

2 Bige, Koločep (map page 57, photograph page 58)
⛴ to Koločep. 55min on foot. Follow Walk 2 (page 57) to **Bige** (❸); return the same way.
A beautiful secluded cove with crystal-clear turquoise water, shaded by tall graceful pines.

3 Svete Ivan, Lopud ○ (map page 60, photograph pages 60-61)
⛴ to Lopud. 20min on foot. Follow Walk 3 (page 59) to **Svete Ivan** (❶); retrace steps to the harbour. The only shade is from the chapel walls.
A short climb to one of the oldest chapels on the island; superb views of islands and mountains to the north.

4 Benešin Rat, Lopud (map page 60, photograph pages 60-61)
⛴ to Lopud. 1h on foot. Follow the promenade (Obala Ivana Kuljevana) round the harbour. Past the hotel and houses, a track leads to a **rotunda** (❾) at the island's south-western wooded tip.
An easy, level stroll to the point, with lovely views of the island of Šipan.

5 Veliji Vrh Vidikovak, Šipan (touring map, no photo)

⛴ to Suđurad. From there catch the local bus to and from Luka; check return times carefully). 1h50min on foot, an easy to moderate walk, with 243m/ 800ft of ascent on paths, tracks, and very quiet roads with signposts. Set out along a lane beside house 93 about 40m to the right of the Information Centre in Luka Šipanska. Nearby is an information board with a map showing the network of paths. Bear left at a fork (3min); pass house 83 Luka on the right and go through an olive grove to a wide concrete path. Bend left beside a derelict building and go up steps to a road. Turn left; keep to this road past two junctions, then go right along a gravel track (33min). After 10 minutes, a distinct path (marked by a small cairn) leads up left to the communications installations on the **Veliji Vrh Vidikovak summit** (55min). Islands dominate the view westward, Mljet being the most prominent. Return the same way. *This is the highest point on the most remote of the Elaphiti islands, with an uncommercialised, old world atmosphere.*

6 St Mary's Island, Mljet (map pages 62-63, photograph page 65)

🚗 (Car tour 1) or ⛴ to Pomena or Polače. The Park entry fee includes boat to the island, north of ❸ on the map. Here you'll find Restaurant Melita, open daily May to end September and an information centre, in the 12th-century Benedictine monastery. At least 30min on foot. Walk up steps to the **Church of the Assumption** of the Blessed Virgin Mary, which should be open, its interior austerely beautiful. It has been a place of pilgrimage for centuries. Then follow a path along the north side of the church, up to the site of some **Roman ruins** and a more recent stable, on the **island's high point**. Descend steps to the lower path and turn right. You pass two small **chapels** (St John and St Benedict) and a **cemetery** and soon find yourself back at the restaurant and ferry jetty. *A picnic or a restaurant lunch in an historic setting where peace and tranquillity acquire new meanings.*

7 Franciscan monastery, Orebić (map page 74, no photo)

🚗 (Car tour 1) or 🚌 to Orebić. 1h10min on foot. Follow Shorter walk 7-1 (page 72) to the 15th-century **Franciscan monastery** and Church of our Lady of the Angels (❸); there is a small museum in the monastery. Possible sunny picnic spots near the monastery. Return the same way. *An undemanding walk up to a first-class vantage point for views of old Korčula town, the scenic local coast and the mountains.*

8 Svete Petar, Makarska (yellow highlighting on the maps on pages 78 and 82, photo overleaf)

🚗 (Car tour 2) or 🚐 to Makarska. 30min on foot. From the marina at the western end of Makarska harbour (◯), walk past Hotel Miramare, then bear right up a minor road which becomes a track below an imposing statue of **Svete Petar**. Continue through pine woodland. From time to time you'll find display boards featuring the colourful work of **Antun Gojak**, a significant 20th-century Makarskan painter. From a junction go up steps and through an archway to **Svete Petar church**, from the 15th century, later rebuilt and renovated. Continue through another archway, then bear left down steps to the shore and turn right. There are plenty of seats on the way to **Svete Petar lighthouse**

(1884), another excellent viewpoint. Nearby is an intriguing installation, under construction at time of writing, using mainly prepared slender pine stems, rope and basket work. Follow the paved path back to the hotel and marina. *Explore the smaller of the two headlands guarding Makarska harbour, and the tranquil setting of Svete Petar church; views of the mountains and islands of Brač and Hvar.*

9 Osejava Forest Park, Makarska (best shown on the map on page 82, photo page 76)

🚗 (Car tour 2) or 🚌 to Makarska. 55min on foot. Walk south along the promenade (Ulica Marineta), past a car park and across to wide steps on the seaward side of Hotel Osejava. On a bend go right up steps below a house. At a junction turn right along the wider upper trail in open pine woodland. Continue up to the **meteorological station** and communications tower and follow the trail to the left. At an intersection go straight on, then on a left bend, go right, just past an information board featuring the forest park. Descend to a junction (35min) with benches for a picnic. Here you have a choice. Either turn right, or turn left to **Plaža Nugal**, a small, peaceful cliff-lined beach, FKK in season and another picnic venue (add 30 minutes and return to the junction to continue along the broad path ahead). Soon there's a 10m-long rope barrier on the left above a sheer drop, but there's no danger! Go past a junction below the communications tower and, at the next junction turn left, after 300m rejoining your outward path, and so back to the start. *Osejava, the wooded headland southwest of Makarska's harbour, is a cool*

Svete Petar peninsula (Picnic 8)

haven on a warm day, with superb views of the harbour and Brač.

10 Vidova Gora, Brač ○ (map page 90, photograph page 91)

🚗 (Car tour 3). 20min on foot. From the car park at the end of the road to Vidova Gora, walk up the road to the **summit** (**7**) with its masts, large cross and a restaurant with one of the finest outlooks imaginable. On the way up, there are sunny picnic spots to the left of the road, close to the plateau rim. The panoramic view embraces the islands of Vis, Hvar, Korčula and Lastovo (poking up above Korčula); the Biokovo range, Pelješac peninsula, and Bol and Zlatni Rat below. *Magnificent views from the highest summit in the Adriatic islands.*

11 Uvala Podstine, Hvar ○ (yellow highlighting on the map on pages 98-99, no photo)

🚗 (Car tour 4) or 🚢 and 🚌 to

Hvar town. Up to 1h on foot from Hvar town. Walk westwards from Trg Svete Stepana, around shady Šumica headland to **Bonj** (safe swimming). It's now much quieter as you continue around Majerovica headland, past Uvala Majerovica, and round Punta Kovać to the entrance to **Uvala Podstine**. There are numerous seats and gently sloping rocks en route, suitable for picnics.
Fine views of the Pakleni islands, yachts plying the channel, and the high coastal cliffs northwest of Uvala Podstine.

12 Španjola Fort, Hvar town ○ (yellow highlighting on the map on pages 98-99, photo page 21)

🚗 (Car tour 4) or ⛴ and 🚌 to Hvar town. 50min on foot, with 102m/325ft ascent. From Trg Svete Stepana, almost opposite Hvar's historic public theatre, follow **Kroz Grodu**, a wide path

leading to 157 steps (I counted them!) up between restaurants then houses; cross a road and go through an archway into **Dr Josip Avelini Park** and more steps. Near the town wall, on a left bend, go through an arch and up to the wall of **Španjola**. Cross the car park to the entrance on the right (entry fee); the fort is open from about 9am to dusk; there's an information board just inside.
Climb to the historic 16th-century fortress for excellent views from several vantage points on the walls; choose between a picnic or the café at the fort. Inspect the museum and prison.

13 Glavica, Stari Grad (Hvar) ○ (yellow highlighting on the map on page 96, no photo)

🚗 (Car tour 4) or 🚌 from Hvar town to Stari Grad. 37min on foot, with 111m/364ft ascent on quiet roads, tracks and paths. From the Tourist Office, follow Put

Skradinski Buk in the Krka National Park (Picnic 18)

Kardinala past the school. Then turn right with a sign to VIEWPOINT GLAVICA along Ulica Ivana Mestrovica. Further up, around a bend, this becomes Ulica Kralja Tomislava. Within 75m diverge up a track marked by a crucifix sign. About 200m further on, continue on a path through woodland to reach the **Glavica summit**, a large cross, tiny chapel and numerous benches and plenty of picnic spots. Prominent in the wide view is Stari Grad Plain to the east (see Walk 15, page 96). Retrace steps to Stari Grad.

An easy ascent to a small chapel on a hill overlooking Stari Grad, prominent in its history since prehistoric times; fine coast and mountain views.

14 Ceška Vila, Vis town (touring map)

🚗 (Car tour 5) or ⛴ to Vis town. 1h50min on foot, with minimal ascent, on paths and quiet streets. Follow the promenade from the small park just east of the ferry terminal. About 70m past a small park on the right, diverge to the right along narrow Ulica Ivana Farolfija then Ulica Vladimira Nazora for about 250m. At a T-junction, fork left along the same street. With shops on both sides, bear left along a lane to the shore. Skirt the small harbour, to come to a square with restaurants and date palms. At the far end, beside Jaska Palace, go up steps and turn first left. Soon you're back at sea level. The road ends near the small 9th-century **Church of St George** (Vis town's patron saint), normally locked. Behind it is the walled **English Graveyard** with the graves of British servicemen killed in action near Vis in 1812 and 1943-45. Facing the cemetery, bear left up shallow steps and cross an open flat area to a path above the shore; the beach is nearby to the right. The path skirts the headland, passing a variety of potential picnic spots, and leads to **Ceška Vila**. The derelict three-storey building was acquired by a Czechoslovak family (hence the name Ceška

Vila), commandeered by the army during World War II, and occupied by them until the late 1980s. Retrace your steps to Vis town. *The small pine-clad headland on the eastern side of the entrance to Vis harbour is one of the prettier places on the island, with its rocky shore, tall pines and a secluded shingle beach. Here you'll also find an historic cemetery and a forlorn, once-handsome villa.*

15 Svete Blaž, Komiža, Vis (touring map, photo pages 22-23)

🚗 (Car tour 5) or ⛴ to Vis town, 🚌 to Komiža. 1h40min on foot, with 240m/790ft ascent, on paths and quiet streets. From the bus stop, go uphill and around a bend on Ulica Komiških Iseljenika, past the car park. At an intersection, turn right along Ulica Dom M Pavlinoviča. From its end continue straight on along an unsignposted path which gains height through low scrubland. At a junction turn left and keep on up to **Svete Blaž** (55min). Solidly stone-built, it dates from at least the 16th century; although normally locked you can see its simple, well-kept interior through the small windows. Retrace steps to the start. *A steady climb along a clear path to this tiny church with superb views across Komiža and its bay to Mt Hum, the highest point on Vis.*

16 Titova Špilja, Vis (touring map, photograph page 24)

🚗 (Car tour 5). 20min on foot. From the road to Hum climb short flights of steps to a T-junction, passing a large boulder on which is carved an inscription — in Croatian. To the left is a small, partly walled-in cave with a plaque (also only in Croatian) about events in 1944. Return to the junction and continue up to the main cave at **Titova Špilja**, a large overhang partly enclosed by a

stone wall, with a small annexe, on one wall of which is a poem titled 'Nas Voda' (Our Water). A plaque outside describes its significance … in Croatian.

A short climb to the headquarters of Tito's Partisans during 1944, with extraordinary views of the valley below and sea beyond. (See also panel on pages 70-71.) It's possible to walk to Svete Duh (see Picnic 17 below) and back from here (50min; 120m/395ft ascent). Follow the waymarked path indicated by a sign, HUM 1H. *Turn left at a vehicle track, then right to* PANORAMA, *and Svete Duh on the summit.*

17 Svete Duh, Vis (touring map)

🚗 (Car tour 5). 10min on foot. From the road to Hum walk up a rough gravel track to the small 15-century chapel, **Svete Duh**, perched on an outlier of Mount Hum. At 563m, it is just a little lower than the mountaintop itself (587m). Hum, a military communications site, is out of bounds. *Almost on top of the island, with fine views to the north and west.*

18 Krka National Park (touring map, photograph opposite)

🚗 (Car tour 2, Itinerary 2). Up to 1 hour on foot. In Skradin buy your national park ticket at the park office near the shore. Catch the national park boat (hourly service) to the park entrance upstream near **Skradinski Buk**. From here you can follow a circuit around the clearly signposted paths and boardwalks, past lookouts over the lakes and waterfalls (17 in all), across rushing streams and past tranquil ponds. There are several information boards, bistros, food and souvenir stalls, picnic areas and toilets along the way. To extend your visit to a full day, choose between boat trips upriver to beautiful **Roški Slap** waterfall, **Visovac Island** and its Franciscan monastery, or **Krka monastery** and fortress ruins. Enquire at the park office for details.

Krka National Park protects 2km of the course of the Krka River and the lower reaches of its tributary, the Čikola, along which there are more than 25 waterfalls with a total drop of 242m. The outstanding highlights of the park are the **travertine formations** between the falls and pools, similar to those in Plitvice Lakes National Park (see panel on page 105). The park also protects a very diverse flora and fauna, and prehistoric sites and buildings from Roman times to the recent past. For more information see www.npkrka.hr.

From near **Skradinski Buk**, where the boat deposits you, turn right at the former entry station and, beyond a thicket of food and souvenir traps, cross the bridge in front of the superb spectacle of **Skradinski Buk**, the classic Krka waterfall. Go up flights of stone steps, past a former power station, to a viewpoint. As elsewhere, follow WALK THIS WAY signs. Bear right across an open area and up to an even better viewpoint. Continue to a road and turn left, soon reaching an **Ethno Souvenir shop** and working water mills. Beyond a small lake go left along a board-walk. You then cross an uninter-rupted, miraculous succession of streams, small cascades and ponds, many harbouring shoals of fish and where you'll hear, if not see, very vociferous frogs. Past signposted **Marasovica Lake** on the left there's a lookout, then steps and boardwalks take you back to the momentarily unreal world of food and souvenir stalls near the bridge. The ferry is not far to the right.
Awesomely beautiful waterfalls and lakes, close-up views of miraculous travertine formations and their wildlife.

19 Veliki Slap, Plitvice Lakes (map page 106, photograph page 26)

🚗 (Car tour 6, Itinerary 1) or 🚐 to Plitvice Lakes National Park. 45min on foot. See Short walk 18, page 104. Before or after the walk, take advantage of one of the picnic tables on the open **grassy area** beyond the jetty overlooking **Jezero Kozjak** (near ⬤).
An outstandingly scenic walk to Croatia's highest waterfall, with magnificent views of some of the lakes.

20 Paclaric fort and viewpoint ○ (yellow highlighting on the map on page 111)

🚗 (Car tour 6, Itinerary 1) or 🚐 to Starigrad-Paklenica (see Walk 19). 40min on foot, with about 70m/230ft ascent. From the lower car park, walk up the road to a sign on the right to VIEWPOINT and EDUCATIONAL TRAIL. Cross a bridge to the **restored mill**, inside which is information about the history of milling locally and the restored mill with grindstone and grain feeder. Uphill from the mill a well-made trail to HISTORICAL VIEW rises fairly steeply, past large information boards about the caravan route through the gorge, traditional agriculture, livestock breeding and houses. Go past the fragile remains of the fort to the lookout and learn about its strategic importance and the features in the view. See also Picnic 21 below.
An opportunity to learn about the park's natural features and local history, in exceptionally scenic surroundings.

21 Večko Kula ○ (yellow high-lighting on the map on page 111, photograph page 25)

🚗 (Car tour 6, Itinerary 1) or 🚐 to Starigrad-Paklenica. 1h10min on foot. Start from a bend on the main D8 road at the junction with a minor road leading to National Park Paklenica and a campsite. Maps and souvenirs are available at the nearby park office. Follow the roadside path south-east, passing

11th-century **Svete Petar** on the left, Starigrad-Paklenica's oldest church. Turn right in front of the *SELINE* sign to *PLAZA, VECKO KULA*. A tariff is payable at the parking area. Follow a wide brick-paved

Mirila graves (Picnic 22)

path, past a shingle beach and through a neatly landscaped area with picnic tables and children's play areas. Beyond a bridge, continue on a wide track to **Večko Kula**, with information about its history up to the 17th century by which time it was in ruins. The best place for a picnic is near the start of a wide track which leads to an informal car park from where you return to the main road and back to Starigrad-Paklenica. See also Picnic 20 above.

Wonderful views of Velika Paklenica and Mala Paklenica from the remains of a 16th-century tower built to guard the Velibitski Kanal.

22 Mirila, Starigrad-Paklenica (yellow highlighting on the map on page 111, photograph page 41)

🚗 (Car tour 6). 2.6km; 1h20min on foot, with 250m/820ft ascent. From the main D8 road opposite Marin restaurant, walk up Put Binara, signposted to MIRILA STONE MONUMENTS. At a T-junction turn left then first right (both turns signposted) and go steeply up Ulica Alojzija Stepnica. Continue straight ahead along a wide track, across an intersection, and follow a path up through pine forest. The way is clearly marked, soon in the open, over rocky ground, overlooked by steep, rugged hillsides. The gradient eventually eases and you reach a wide, partly **grassy amphitheatre**. Helpful information is on a board to your right. The Mirila (memorial stones) are arranged in four closely packed clusters; most are small and short and many bear distinctive carvings. Retrace steps to the start.

A straightforward climb to a traditional 'resting place of the soul'. This unique funeral practice was followed by mountain communities, from the 17th-20th centuries. Flat stones, many bearing special markings, represented the height of the deceased who were buried elsewhere.

23 Komrčar Park and Rab old town (yellow highlighting on the map on page 135, photographs pages 29 and 135)

🚗 (Car tour 7, Itinerary 3) or 🚢 and 🚌 to Rab town. 55min on foot. With your back to the harbour, leave Trg Svete Kristofora (distinguished by a fountain and black metallic sculpture) along a wide path to the right — immediately to the right of two date palms. This takes you into **Komrčar Park**, created between 1883 and 1905 on the site of the old town pasture. The most common trees are Aleppo pine, together with black pine, laurel, Italian cypress, holm oak, palms and agaves. Ignore all junctions until you're close to a cemetery gate; turn left and start to descend. Go straight on to steps which lead down to the shore beside a bar (20min). Similar to Obalno Setalište Franza Josefa (Walk 22, page 118), this promenade was built to mark royal enthusiasm for the coast, here Prince Alois of Leichtenstein who visited in 1910 and sponsored the path's construction. Follow the broad path to the left; beside and near the path there are plenty of **shaded seats and places to swim**. With a massive wall topped by old buildings rising directly from the water 20m ahead, climb steps to Trg Slobode (40min), dominated by a large holm oak. This is Liberty Square, commemorating liberation from Italian occupation in 1921. Cross and turn right along Ulica Ivana Rabljanina, past the Benedictine monastery **Svete Andrije**, then past 12th-century **St Mary's campanile** (open daily) to **Rab Cathedral** (Church of the

Holy Virgin Mary's Assumption), of ancient origin. Turn right to skirt the church, then right again, past small **Svete Antun monastery church** (1494). Turn left down a path to **Kaldanac Park**, with a statue of Svete Marin, a local and founder of the Republic of San Marino. Go through an archway on your right to the road, cross and turn left, back to the start.
A varied and scenic stroll through wooded parkland, along the shore of Uvala Svete Eufemija and back through the old town and its fascinating old churches and monasteries.

24 Baška, Krk (map page 148, photograph pages 138-139)

🚗 (Car tour 7, Itinerary 2) or 🚌 to Baška on Krk. 1h8min or 1h12min on foot. Follow Walk 32 (page 147) to the 34min-mark at ❹ or the 36min-mark, where you could picnic close to or below the path.
Superb views of Baška and its bay, the wide valley between the surrounding mountains, and out to sea.

25 Mrtvaška, Lošinj (touring map)

🚗 (Car tour 8, Itinerary 3). 4min on foot. Walk through the lower car park at **Mrtvaška** to reach a small shingle **beach** with some shade. Note that the waymarked path to the right is rough and doesn't lead to any nearby beaches. Alternatively (or additionally), there are seats and a picnic table beside **Svete Ivan** church, with a great view of Veli Lošinj and the sea beyond. It's best visited on the way back from Mrtvaška — see the Car touring notes and allow 5min on foot.
Island vistas from the rocky coast at the southern tip of Lošinj; panoramic views from an historic chapel perched above Veli Lošinj.

26 Veli Lošinj harbour (map page 158, photograph pages 158-159)

🚗 (Car tour 8) or 🚢 to Cres and 🚌 to Veli Lošinj. 10min on foot. Follow Walk 36 (see page 157) from the harbour as far as the **Rotonda** (just before ❶); along the way there are **benches** beside the path and a **small park** just above.
An easy stroll to shady, scenic outlooks over the busy harbour.

27 Lungomare, Cres town (map page 161, photographs pages 160 and 162-163)

🚗 (Car tour 9) or 🚢 and 🚌 to Cres town. 1h40min on foot, with negligible ascent on paved paths (beware cycists!). On the north side of Cres harbour, set out along Palada (a street), soon turning the corner into **Lungomare Svete Mikule**. The path leads to a beach spread round a small headland, **Rt Kovačine** (❽); the Blue Flag beach, **Plaža Kampa Kovačine**, extends northwards from here. The narrower path leads on through an area designated FKK (naturist), though apparently not exclusively so in practice. Just past **Gavza** you come to an Area of Centuries Old Olive Groves (see also Walk 37, page 163). The concrete path ends above **Uvala Gavza** (❼), a pretty shingle cove. A path leads on to the end of the **headland** along the northern side of the bay; there are some excellent picnic sites along here. Retrace steps to Cres town.
The 'lungomare' is a classic feature of several seaside towns — the habitat of strollers, seeing and being seen. Cres town's lungomare, popular with families and close to the town, leads past many bars, restaurants and swimming opportunities at one of Croatia's many Blue Flag beaches to a lovely sheltered cove.

Continues overleaf

28 Valun, Cres (touring map, photograph page 143)

🚗 (Car tour 9, Itinerary 1). 10-15min on foot. Park just past the 30 sign or about 100m further on at the left (free parking at time of writing). Parking is *not* permitted in the village. Walk straight down to the shore. Turn left for the more popular of Valun's two beaches. To the right are restaurants, a mini-market, and a smaller, quieter, safe beach. At **Konoba Tos Juna** you'll find examples of Glagolitic tablets, pottery and plaques. In the prominent **Church of St Mary** there is a replica of an 11th-century bilingual tombstone found in the former hamlet of Bućev, the inhabitants of which moved to the coast to found Valun. It is the earliest surviving example of the Croatian language in the Glagolitic script. (See 'Glagolitic script panel on page 143.)

A delightful, isolated village with two superb beaches — a million miles from almost anywhere.

29 Lubenice (touring map, photograph page 32)

🚗 (Car tour 9, Itinerary 1). Up to 25min on foot. A few steps from the car park is a truly **breathtaking view** almost directly down to the small beach of **Sv Ivan**, accessible only by a very steep, rough path. Lubenice's history stretches back over 4000 years, though today it has only a handful of residents. Wander through the village's cobbled streets, past many remarkably intact old buildings, including a 15th-century church, to vantage points (and potential picnic sites) above and beyond the **church and graveyard**, with magnificent views northwards —

the Učka mountain range is particularly impressive. There is also a small **museum** devoted to sheep breeding and associated folklore.

Explore an old village, in an awesome clifftop location; sample local products; picnic — or dine at a small courtyard restaurant.

30 Sis ○ (touring map, photograph page 31)

🚗 (Car tour 9, Itinerary 2). 1h45min on foot, with 278m/912ft of ascent on a clear, sign-posted and waymarked path. See 'Equipment' on page 47, and take walking poles. From the northern end of the concrete wall at the turn-off to **Beli** from the Cres town–Porozina road a clear path leads up beside a stone wall on the left. The slope is carpeted with very aromatic wild sage from late spring. Stunted oaks and hornbeam provide some shade. Just before reaching a transverse wall (50min), bear left across boulders up to a large cairn on **Sis** (the nearby summit is monopolised by a rusted derelict building). The view is extraordinary, including the Velebit range on the mainland, Istria, the islands of Rab, Krk and Pag, and the village of Valun (Picnic 28). Take care when leaving the summit: way-markers may be faint and sparse. As you descend eastwards, the path soon becomes clear. Watch for the left turn through the wall, then retrace your steps to the road.

A comparatively short climb through masses of wild sage to magnificent views from Sis (639m) the second highest point on Cres. Gorice (648m), the highest point, is further north and inaccessible.

Walking

Croatia's coast, the nearby mountains, and many of the islands — from one end of the Adriatic Sea to the other — offer a remarkable variety of walks. They range from easy strolls along promenades — in the best Mediterranean tradition of the *passegiata*, to energetic ascents of spectacular mountain peaks. Many of the walks follow ancient paths and trails through beautiful beech and oak forests, olive groves and vineyards where the rocky countryside has been laboriously terraced to make cultivation possible. You may find yourself in landscapes where little has changed for centuries — not least the skilfully built paths, which still make traversing rough ground fairly easy. Some walks pass or visit sites bearing witness to the abiding significance of religious belief, others to the country's long, often turbulent history. The magnificently scenic coast is intricately indented with innumerable coves and beaches, supremely peaceful, seemingly remote, yet easily accessible.

This book features 37 main walks, some with alternatives, and almost all with at least one shorter version. They are grouped by island, by national or nature park, or by the most convenient base. Eleven islands, four national parks, two nature parks, the Pelješac peninsula and the Makarska Riviera are covered. In the 'Picnics and short walks' section you will find another 16 walks ranging in duration from 45 minutes to 1h50min. With a total of 90 long and short walks, this book should suit all tastes and abilities. Whichever walks you choose, I hope they whet your appetite and that you will return to this ceaselessly fascinating country and its exceptionally beautiful and diverse landscapes.

Grading, waymarking, maps, GPS

The walks are **graded** according to distance, amount of ascent, roughness of the going underfoot and specific challenges. There is a quick overview of each walk's grade in the Contents. In the Contents the grade assigned is generalised in favour of the lower grade, eg some parts of moderate walks may be easy. The introductory remarks provide more detailed information. Here is a brief overview of the four gradings:

● easy — more or less level (perhaps with a short climb to a viewpoint); good surfaces underfoot; easily followed

● easy-moderate — ascents/descents of no more than 300m/1000ft; good surfaces underfoot; easily followed

● moderate-strenuous — ascents/descents may be over 500m/1800ft; variable surfaces underfoot — you must be sure-footed and agile; possible route-finding problems in poor visibility

● very strenuous — only suitable for very experienced hillwalkers with a head for heights; difficult terrain underfoot. None of the walks in this book require rock climbing skills and only two have a short section of fixed rope.

Half the main walks are graded blue, almost one-third are red, and the rest green.

Signposting on Walk 5

All the walks follow paths, trails or tracks, almost all of which are **signposted and/or way-marked** with paint marks, usually red and white strips or circles; other colours appear occasionally.

The **maps** in this book are based on Openstreetmap mapping (see page 2). Most are at the scale 1:50,000 and are adequate for the walks described, but if you wish to venture further afield, you should obtain the relevant map (see details at the top of each walk for my suggestions) and, possibly, a compass or GPS tracks from a reliable source. Routes of other walks are also shown on many of the brochures available from tourist information and national park offices, and from The Map Shop (see page 8) for SMAND and Croatian Mountain Rescue Service maps.

Free **GPS tracks** are available for all these walks: see the Croatia page on the Sunflower website. Please bear in mind, however, that GPS readings should *never* be relied upon as your sole reference point. Conditions can change at any time. Those of you who don't use GPS on the ground may nevertheless enjoy opening the GPX files in Google Earth to preview the walks in advance!

Equipment and safety
For each walk, only *special equipment* is mentioned, eg walking poles, and whether walking shoes or trekking sandals will be suitable. The contents of your pack must take

account of the weather, time of the year and length of the walk.

• Always carry plenty of food and water.
• Wear good walking boots on all walks except where indicated.
• Always carry extra clothing, including a waterproof jacket, even on warm days. Extra items are essential for mountain walks.
• Take sun protection cream, sunglasses and a shady hat.
• Carry a basic first-aid kit.

Extra equipment for mountain walks:
• Waterproof jacket and trousers
• Windproof jacket and/or fleece top
• Warm hat and gloves
• Map, compass, whistle, GPS or smartphone (or mobile). The emergency number for medical help, fire, police, mountain and coastguard rescue is 112, but remember that mobiles may not be universally reliable.

Safety
• Estimate your ability conservatively.
• Avoid walking alone; leave word of your intended route and check in when you return.
• Turn back if the route proves too difficult or if the weather deteriorates — thunderstorms can develop very quickly, especially in summer.
• Choose a low-level walk if storms are forecast.
• Remember that the ubiquitous limestone rock becomes *very* slippery when wet.
• Take care on rocky paths across steep mountain slopes. Try to avoid knocking stones off the path; if this happens, always shout a warning to anyone below.

Weather

Croatia's coast and islands enjoy a Mediterranean climate: hot, dry summers and mild, damp winters (snow is, however, common down to low levels). During July and August maximum **temperatures** exceed 30°C almost daily — generally too hot for safe and comfortable walking, except in the early morning and evening. Vigorous **thunderstorms** and heavy downpours seem to occur in a pattern after several warm days, as the humidity rises and the visibility becomes very hazy.

Winds from particular directions are a distinctive feature of the weather, so much so that they have specific names. Of these, the one you're most likely to encounter is the *bura* that roars in from the northeast with incredible ferocity, whipping up clouds of spray at sea and making walking normally quite difficult. The *bura* is most common during winter, but I have experienced it during early summer and early autumn. Winds

from the south often bring cloud and rain, while the south-easterly *široko* is warm and dry. The *maestral*, a pleasant sea breeze, can bring welcome relief during the morning and early afternoon.

Weather forecasts can sometimes be found in official tourist information offices or harbour-masters' offices. The Meteorological Service of Croatia's website gives forecasts for many of the towns in this book: www.meteo.hr/index.en.

The best times to visit Croatia for walking are late April to early June, and September to mid-October.

Where to stay

All the walks start from a town or village with a choice of accommodation listed under '**Nearest accommodation**' at the start of the walk. The Croatian National Tourist Office has links to local tourist information offices and agencies for accommodation in **hotels, self-catering apartments** and **private homes**. **Camping** sites are plentiful, from small simple sites in secluded locations to large sites resembling small villages in their range of facilities. **Youth and private hostels** are confined to cities and some popular towns.

Nuisances

Several species of **snakes** live in Croatia, including two that are venomous: the horn-nosed viper (*Vipera ammodytes*) and the common viper (*Vipera berus*). Two species are semi-venomous, the rest harmless and decorative. None are lethal for normally healthy people. I saw specimens of at least three species in various places, enjoying the sun on a warm rock, but which slithered away at the first hint of my presence, one obviously confused by blind alleys in a well-built stone wall. The chances of being bitten are extremely remote, especially if you're wearing ankle-high boots, thick socks and, preferably, long trousers. If the worst should happen, then disturb the patient as little as possible and seek medical help without delay.

Country code

Please keep all the following points in mind as you walk.
- Keep to paths and trails.
- Heed warning and advisory signs.
- Do not pick plants, collect shells, or disturb birds and animals.
- Do not damage signs or visitors' books.
- Avoid causing rock falls.

Left: beautiful Dubrovnik is a good base for both touring and walking and is easily reached from Britain by charter and budget flights.

- Leave gates as you find them.
- Keep dogs under control; do not take them into national parks.
- Do not light fires, drop cigarette butts or lighted matches in forests.
- Take all your litter home.
- Greet local people with 'Dobar dan'; for other walkers: 'Dobar dan/ Gruss Gott/Guten tag/Hello/Ciao' will almost always draw a response.

Croatian for walkers

Croatian is a Slavonic language and, at first sight, a seemingly impenetrable jumble of consonants occasionally separated by vowels. But it is easy to pronounce, so it's not difficult to learn a few basic phrases and words, always appreciated by the locals. However, English is very widely spoken, especially by people under the age of about 30 and in tourist offices and travel agencies. German is also in common use, especially on the islands of Brač, Hvar, Rab and Krk. Below is a simple guide to pronunciation and some basic words and phrases you may need while walking or touring.

pronunciation of vowels		*pronunciation of consonants*	
a	as in father	c	as in pits
aj	as in aisle	ć č	as in chilli
e	as in set	dz Đ đ	as in jelly
i	as in tree	j	as in youth
o	as in saw	lj	as in bullion
oj	as in toy	nj	as in canyon
u	as in took	r	rolled slightly
		š	as in shell
		ž	as in treasure

A few useful phrases and words

Hello	Dobar dan
Good morning	Dobro jutro
Good evening	Dobro večer
Goodbye	Doviđenja
Please; I beg your pardon	Molim
Thank you	Hvala
Yes. No	Da. Ne
You're welcome	Nema na čemu
Do you speak English?	Govorite li engleski?
Help!	Upomoć!
I'm lost	Izgubio sam se
Where is?	Gdje je?
How far is it?	Koliko daleko je?
I understand	Razumijem
I don't understand	Ja ne razumijem
Please write it down	Možete li molim vas to napisati
straight ahead	ravno
left/right	lijevo/desno
near/far	blizu/daleko
early/late	jani/kasan

easy/difficult	lako/teško
little/big	malo/veliko
open/closed	otvoreno/zatvoreno
north/east/south/west	sjever/istok/jug/zapad
toilets	zahod
restaurant	konoba/restoran/gostionica
cake and ice cream shop	slastičarnica
hotel/guest house	hotel/pansion
hostel/camping	gostionica/kamp
drinking water	voda

Here are some other useful words, including those found on maps and in the text.

Croatian	English	English	Croatian
Brdo/breg	hill	administration/ office	uprava
brod	boat/ship	bay	uvala
buk	cascade	beach	plaža
cesta	road	boat/ship	brod
crkva	church	bridge	most
dolina	valley	car ferry	trajekt
dom	house	cascade	buk
draga	shallow valley	castle	dvorac
dvorac	castle	cave	špilja/pećina
FKK	naturist/nudist	cemetery	groblje
gora/gorje	massif	church	crkva
grmljavina	thunderstorm	crag	kuk
groblje	cemetery	field	polje
izvor	spring	forest	šuma
jezero	lake	harbour	luka
karta	map	headland	rt/rat
kiša	rain	hiking/walking	pješačenje
krš	karst (limestone)	holidays	praznikom
		hill	brdo/breg
kuća	house	house	dom/kuca
kuk	crag	island	otok
kula	castle	karst/limestone	krš
luka	harbour	lake	jezero
more	sea	lane	put
most	bridge	lighthouse	svjetionik
obala	waterfront/ promenade	lookout	vidikovak
otok	island	map	karta
pješačenje	hiking/walking	massif	gora, gorje
planina	mountain	monastery	samostan
plaža	beach	mountain	planina
polje	field	naturist/nudist	FKK
potok	stream	pass	sedlo/prijevoj
put	trail/lane	path	setalište, staza
rijeka	river	promenade	obala

rt/rat	headland	rain	kiša
samostan	monastery	river	rijeka
sedlo/prijevo	pass	road	cesta
šetalište	path/walkway	sea	more
slap	waterfall	spring	izvor
špilja/pećina	cave	square	trg
staza	path	stream	potok
šuma	forest	street	ulica
sunce	sun	summit	vrh
svjetionik	lighthouse	sun	sunce
trajekt	car ferry	thunderstorm	grmljavina
trg	square	trail	put
ulica	street	valley	dolina
uprava	administration/ office	valley (shallow)	draga
uvala	bay	viewpoint	vidikovak
vidikovak	lookout/viewpoint	walkway	šetalište
vjetar	wind	waterfall	slap/vodopad
vodopad	waterfall	waterfront	obala
vrh	summit	weekday/ workday	radnim/danom
		wind	vjetar

Organisation of the walks

The walks are **grouped** according to the car tour from which they are accessible, by individual walking bases, islands or national parks, and from south (Dubrovnik) to north (Rijeka). This is shown on the fold-out touring map. Each walk starts from a town or village and can be reached by public transport. The walks are circular, linear and out and back.

At the top of each walk you will find essential information: distance and *walking time (without stops)*, grade, equipment, transport, nearest accommodation and, in almost all cases, alternative shorter walks. *Do check your walking times against mine on a short walk before venturing on a long hike.*

Below is a key to the symbols on the walking maps.

▬▬▬ trunk road	↠ spring, waterfall	▮ castle, fort
▬▬ secondary road	✕ restaurant	∩ cave
▨ minor, town or unmade road	⛪ monastery.church	✕ quarry
▬▬ jeep track	⛪ chapel.cross, shrine	△ campsite
---- path, trail	◐❹ walk start, waypoint	▪ building
—2→ main walk	⊣ cemetery	✝ mountain refuge
—2→ alternative walk	⊓ picnic tables	⚑ monument
—2→ adjacent walk	▣ best views	Å transmitter, mast
---- short 'picnic' walk	🚌 bus stop	P picnic suggestion
—400— height in metres	🚗 car parking	✳ mill
	🚢 ferry port	▮ tower

ELAPHITI ISLANDS: **Introduction**

Conventionally, this small archipelago between Dubrovnik and Mljet embraces Koločep, Lopud and Šipan (and 10 uninhabited islets); the name is derived from the Greek word for 'deer', suggesting they may once have lived here. Here, we've added tiny Lokrum, closest to Dubrovnik, to ensure it's not overlooked (see Walk 1 overleaf). Walking (and/or cycling) is the only feasible way of getting to know them all beyond the small settlements around their ferry ports, served from Dubrovnik direct and via the other islands. All four support dense pine-oak woodlands; cultivated land on anything more than a domestic scale is confined to Šipan (Short 'picnic' walk 5 on page 35), on a broad plain between its two hamlets.

Lopud is the most populous and has the largest range of facilities; the other three are more peaceful, though not bereft of restaurants, and accommodation (except Lokrum). All four can be explored via a network of paths, signposted more or less helpfully, to viewpoints, historic sites — churches and forts — and beaches. Though the walks described are neither long nor difficult, each island is definitely worth at least a full day's visit.

Photo: Portoč, Lokrum (Picnic 1, Walk 1)

Walk 1 (Lokrum): TOUR OF LOKRUM FROM PORTOČ

Distance/time: 5.1km/3.1mi; 1h40min

Grade: ● easy, with approximately 115m/377ft ascent; on signposted trails and paths

Equipment/map: see page 46; sandals or walking shoes, swimming things, Lokrum Reserve map (1:5,000)

Refreshments: available near the ferry landing, beside The Dead Sea and in the old monastery

Transport: passenger 🚢 from Dubrovnik old town harbour (see page 164). Keep in mind the time of the last departure.

Nearest accommodation: Dubrovnik

Short walk: Southern circuit; 2km/1.2mi; 50min. ● Easy; equipment/access as above. Follow the walk to ❸, then go on to the ferry: leaving the **monastery**, go straight ahead instead of left.

The small wooded island of Lokrum, just 15 minutes from Dubrovnik is, in its northern reaches, a relatively peaceful refuge from the crowds, and a fascinating place to visit in its own right. The rocky coastline is delightful, with small sheltered coves, an unusual natural swimming pool (a depression in the limestone rock hollowed out by water

erosion), and some cliff-lined inlets. A Unesco Special Forest Vegetation Reserve since 1976, Lokrum supports an unusually diverse range of trees and plants, including many Mediterranean and some Australian species. There is plentiful evidence of the island's long and eventful history, dating from the 12th century. It is a No Smoking island; this prohibition and the plentiful fire hydrants testify to the ever-present high fire risk. The main beach is designated FKK, for naturists only. At the Visitor Centre above the jetty you can hire an audio guide to more than a dozen features of interest. Lokrum's intricate network of paths is generally well signposted; nevertheless, there's some potential for confusion, unless of course, you're using the following notes.

Start out just above the ferry wharf at **Portoč** (**O**): bear left along a shady trail signposted to TOILETS. Turn right at a junction towards PIGEONS CAVE and THE

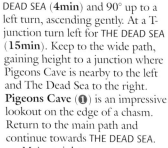

DEAD SEA (**4min**) and 90° up to a left turn, ascending gently. At a T-junction turn left for THE DEAD SEA (**15min**). Keep to the wide path, gaining height to a junction where Pigeons Cave is nearby to the left and The Dead Sea to the right. **Pigeons Cave** (**❶**) is an impressive lookout on the edge of a chasm. Return to the main path and continue towards THE DEAD SEA.

Make a right turn at an unsigned junction with a red fire hydrant, and another at the next, marked junction (**30min**). Dodging the ubiquitous, tame, greedy peacocks, press on to **The Dead Sea**. Here, a few minutes later, is the best opportunity for a swim, but not in wild weather when the surge through a rock fissure turns the Sea into a surfers' delight. For a break, there are seats beside the (real) sea wall on your left.

To continue, go past the playground and, having visited the **monastery** (**❸**), emerge on its eastern side (*from where the Short walk returns*), bear left around it to a junction beside the **Church of the Annunciation**; the plain interior is visible through a barred window. From here you can

The Benedictine monastery

explore the **botanical garden** (**④**; **40min**), home to a wide variety of exotic species (most are labelled). Since the garden is criss-crossed with paths, it's easiest to return to the entrance and then bear right through an olive grove. At the next three junctions, the destination is FORT ROYAL — right, left and left, initially very steeply, up the so-called **Path of Paradise** to **Fort Royal** (**⑤**; **1h**). Flights of steps take you up to the top and the splendid panoramic view.

Exit on the north side, pass a roofless stone building on the left and go through a gap in a stone wall. Soon signposts direct you towards SKALIKA and LAZARET.

Descend, with a good view of the Old Town walls, to a junction (**1h5min**). Turn right, down to the wall of the unfinished 16th-century **quarantine compound** (**⑥**). Go round a corner to a junction and descend; steps on the left lead to **Skalica** (**⑦**), a small cove with views of a corner of Dubrovnik old town and the Mt Srđ massif, and more picnic and swimming potential (**1h12min**).

Back on the main path, follow it past the **Triton cross** (**⑧**; a memorial to the victims of an 1859 maritime disaster), past steps on the left to another picnic spot (**1h23min**), and back to **Portoč** (**1h40min**).

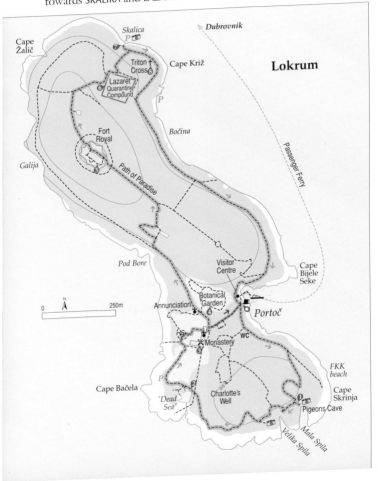

Walk 2 (Koločep): TOUR OF THE ISLAND FROM DONJE ČELO

Distance/time: 3km/1.8mi; 1h25min
Grade: ● easy, with approximately 100m/328ft ascent on very quiet road, trails and paths, with a few signposts and faded waymarkers
Equipment/map: see page 46; walking shoes suitable; Dubrovnik Tourist Board map of Koločep (approximately 1:12,000)
Refreshments: available at Donje Čelo and Gornje Čelo
Transport: passenger 🚢 from Dubrovnik (see page 164)
Nearest accommodation: Donje Čelo, Gornje Čelo, Dubrovnik

Alternative shorter walk (or optional longer walk): Cavalika; 4km/2.4mi; 50min; ● Easy with approximately 50m/164ft ascent. From the junction just below ❶, turn right for CAVALIKA. Initially concrete then unsurfaced, this track leads generally west along the peninsula forming the southern side of the harbour and ends at the western extremity of the island. The views of the harbour, as well as of Lopud and Šipan beyond, are lovely, as is the rich variety of spring wildflowers. Retrace steps to ❶ and either return to Donje Čelo or continue the main walk.

Koločep is the closest to Dubrovnik of the three inhabited Elaphiti islands, where you can experience something of the magical island tranquillity and other-worldness. The rocky coast affords some lovely views, there's a small sheltered beach and a waterside restaurant specialising in locally caught fish.

Start out a few steps from the ferry wharf at **Donje Čelo** (❍): walk up the narrow road called Put Hrv Rat Mornarice between houses and their colourful gardens. Bend right at the medical centre towards *GORNJE ČELO* then, further on, pass a **chapel** (❶; **Svete**

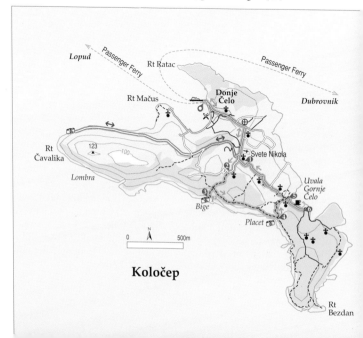

Koločep

Cliffs at Bige

Nikola) and **cemetery**. Where the road bends left, go right for *BIGE* (**14min**). Soon turn left towards *GORNJE CELO* and follow the path (**21min**) past half-hidden derelict buildings and up to a crest in tall pine forest. From a junction on the left here (**24min**), at the corner of a stone wall, descend steeply seawards, soon reaching **Bige** (**❸**; **26min**; Picnic 2), a beautiful, rock-girt cove. You can scramble down to the shore if the crystal-clear water is irresistible. Out to sea the islet of Sveti Andrije floats on the horizon.

Return to the junction above Bige and turn right along a path beside the stone wall; traverse above the cove, then ascend to a crest, with excellent views southwards (**40min**). The path then descends gradually to a clearing. Ignore the trail bending left and follow a narrow path straight on, down through tall pines, to a railed clifftop path at **Placet** (**❹**; **1h**). Steep steps lead down to the rocky shore, perhaps

not an ideal place for a swim, though the nearby coastal cliffs are particularly photogenic.

Retrace steps a short distance to a concrete path on the right and follow it around bends between houses to a **junction with steps on the left** (**❺**); turn right here, to another intersection. Descend steeply on the narrow road to the right, past a small **chapel**, to **Uvala Gornje Čelo** (**1h8min**). There are seats beneath the pines overlooking the small beach, a small hotel to the left and a bar-café along to the right.

Return along the narrow road to the junction at **❺** and bear right up the steps to another junction, where you turn right. Follow this, the island's only main road, past a curious **carved stone slab** set into the stone wall on the left, to the **Svete Nikola chapel** (**❶**) at the junction to Bige and back to **Donje Čelo** and the ferry wharf. There are a couple of bars and an enticing restaurant nearby to the left (**1h25min**).

Walk 3 (Lopud): HIGHLIGHTS OF THE ISLAND FROM UVALA LOPUD

Distance/time: 11.7km/7mi; 3h5min

Grade: ● easy-moderate, with approximately 300m/984ft ascent; on intermittently signposted paths, trails, tracks and quiet roads

Equipment/map: see page 46; boots or walking shoes suitable; Dubrovnik Tourist Board map of Lopud (1:20,000)

Refreshments: available at Uvala Lopud, Plaža Šunj (in summer)

Transport: 🚢 from Dubrovnik to Lopud (see page 164)

Nearest accommodation: Lopud, Dubrovnik

Shorter walks

1 Fortress and Gospa od Šunja;
9.3km/5.7mi; 2h30min. ● Easy, with approximately 250m/820ft ascent; equipment/access as for the main walk. Follow the main walk to the **fortress** and then **Gospa od Šunja**, then return to junction at the 40min-mark and continue towards ŠUNJ BEACH. At the road, bear right to return direct to the start. Alternatively, bear left to Uvala Lopud with the main walk.

2 West coast only; 6.3km/3.8mi; 1h40min. ● Easy, with approximately 200m/656m ascent; equipment etc as for the main walk. Walk round the harbour along Obala Ivana Kuljevana, to a path on the left between a high stone wall and a grove of palms (Ulica od Šunj, signposted to ŠUNJ BEACH). Go past the (no longer) Grand Hotel to a T-junction and turn right; the track soon bends left and climbs, eventually steeply, to a saddle where you join the main walk at the 1h28min mark.

*L*opud's historical heritage is the focus of a network of paths and trails linking some of its many churches and chapels (there were 30 in 1700), a fort built in 1653, together with the rugged west coast. There are signs along Uvala Lopud seafront and inland at many, but not all significant junctions en route to the selected features. However the 'Walking Track' signs lack destinations! A further complication is that vegetation grows, and densely without regular clearing. Nevertheless , do *not* be deterred. With these notes you should not run out of a clear path, nor encounter a jungle. Around the harbour, several bars and restaurants help to make the island an ideal destination for a day out from Dubrovnik, preferably an overnight stay, to really savour its peacefulness after the last ferry has sailed.

The walk starts beside the **Hotel Glavović** (**O**) towards the northern end of **Uvala Lopud**. Follow Ulica Zlatarska between houses and up into the open. At an intersection (**5min**) continue ahjead up Ulica Getina towards FORT/KASTIO. Turn right (**8min**) up steps to **Svete Ivan** (**❶**), a 9th-century Croatian chapel with a superb outlook westward (Picnic 3). Return to the main trail and turn left a few steps further on towards SUTVRAC (fortress; **❷**). Steps and a path lead up to the fort wall, where you bear right to a gateway opening onto the interior of the **fortress** (**❸**; **24min**), affording more fine views, especially towards Dubrovnik.

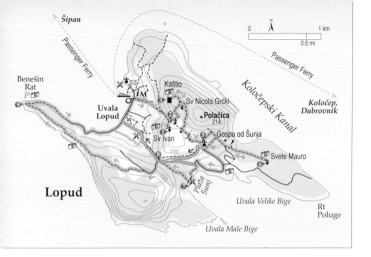

Retrace steps to the junction where you turned left to the fort and bear left past **Svete Nikola Grčki** (**❹**; **30min**). Continue down the path to a trail at a signposted junction opposite a derelict building and turn left

(**37min**). Turn left again at another signposted junction (**40min**).

Turn left again here, to **Gospa od Šunja** (**❺**; **43min**), a remarkable sacred site with a large 15th-century church (open only on

special occasions), chapel, burial ground, and mysterious symbols carved on the paving slabs opposite the church door and elsewhere. *(For Shorter walk 1 follow the sign for ŠUNJ. On reaching the road junction eight minutes later, turn left for the beach or right to Lopud harbour.)*

To continue the main walk, follow a path between the chapel and the enclosing wall, to a junction where you turn right on a trail signed POLUGE/WALKING TRAIL. Then go left at a T-junction along a concrete trail (**47min**). After a few minutes fork right down a path unofficially marked TREKKING WAY (to the left you'd find 'domestic food'). The path could be slightly overgrown for a few metres, then should be clear to the chapel of **Svete Mauro** (**6**; **1h**).

With its stone pews, and stabilised to prevent its collapse, the chapel still has an aura of sanctity.

Unfortunately the onward path is likely to be overgrown, so return to Gospa od Šunja and follow the rough road round and down to the **Šunj Beach** (**7**; **1h20min**), with its atmospheric bars. Leave the beach at its far end along a path signposted WALKING TRACK. This pleasant woodland route climbs to a **saddle** (**8**; **1h30min**). *(Shorter walk 2 joins here.)* Turn left here, up an unmarked track opposite a tall concrete pillar. *(Shorter walk 2 turns right.)* Follow the track up, bearing left at a fork where an informal sign points to BENES/VIDIKOVAC. The track climbs through woodland and soon begins to descend. Pass a quixotic building (which may still be under construction).

Continue past minor path junctions, soon coming to the first of several quite comfortable **seats** (**2h11min** to **2h25min**; some shaded, some not), sited for the spectacular vistas of coastal cliffs and the islands. Descend to a rotunda-style building at **Benešin Rat**, the western tip of the island (**9**; **2h34min**; Picnic 4). From here **Obala Ivana Kuljevana**, a surfaced trail which becomes a road, leads around the shore past the incongruous **Lafodia Hotel** back to the harbour at **Uvala Lopud** and the cluster of bars and restaurants (**3h5min**).

Left: Lopud harbour (Picnics 3 and 4), with the monastery in the background

Walk 4 (Mljet): ZAKAMENICA VIEWPOINT AND VRATOSOLINA FROM POMENA OR POLAČE

See also photo on page 71
Distance/time: 13km/7.8mi; 3h55min (from Pomena); 15km/9mi; 4h36min (from Polače)
Grade: ● easy-moderate (90m/295ft ascent from Pomena, 170m/558ft ascent from Polače). On clear paths, tracks and quiet roads from Pomena; short stretches on quiet roads, and tracks from Polače; signposting.
Equipment/map: see page 46; walking shoes suitable; swimming things; Nakladnik map of Mljet National Park (1:14,000)
Refreshments: available at Pomena, Polače, and at Babine Kuce on the Pomena route
Transport: ⛴ ferry or catamaran to Mljet (see page 164), then on foot from Pomena or Polače
Nearest accommodation: Pomena, Polače

Shorter walks
1 Malo Jezero circuit; 3.9km/2.3mi; 1h15min (from Pomena); 9km/5.4mi; 2h45min (from Polače). ● Easy, with approximately 60m/197ft of ascent from Pomena, ● 140m/459ft ascent from Polače; equipment and transport as for the main walk.
From Pomena follow the main walk to **Mali Most (❶)** and a picnic area. Cross the bridge and turn left. About 200m beyond the head of an inlet, turn left down a path to the shore. Follow it to an informal boat landing. Go up steps to the unsurfaced road and continue up the nearby steps on the right (**ⓐ**), back to **Pomena**.
From Polače follow the main walk to **Mali Most (❶)**, then the notes for Shorter walk 1 above to the steps at the turn-off for Pomena.

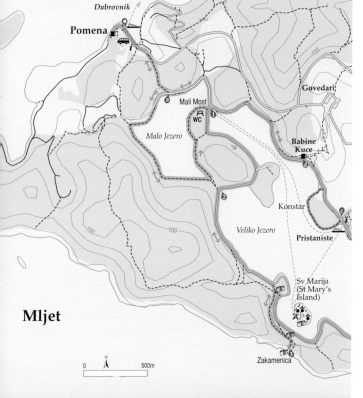

Mljet

Ignore this turn-off; continue all the way around **Malo Jezero** and back to **Mali Most** (**1**), then retrace your steps to **Polače**.
2 Zakamenica only; 7km/4.2mi; 2h20min (from Pomena); 13km/ 7.8mi, 4h (from Polače). ● Easy; equipment and transport as above. Follow the main walk to the **Zakamenica** viewpoint (1h5min from **Pomena**; 1h56min from **Polače**) and return by the same route.

The ever-changing patterns of light and shade on the turquoise waters of the lakes, lovely, serene views of St Mary's Island, an exhilarating lookout on the south coast, the restless surge of the sea at the lakes' outlet, dense woodland, and wind-pruned coastal vegetation combine to make this a walk of great contrasts. Go prepared for a swim, or at least a paddle, near Vratosolina.

To start from Pomena, walk from the quay (**O**) to the eastern end of the village, where a **national park sign** points the way up a flight of stone steps. Follow these up through pine woods and down to a trail overlooking **Malo Jezero** (**a**; **8min**), where you turn right. A few minutes more bring you to an unmarked junction: bear left here, down to the water's edge. The path, rocky at first, soon takes you through trees and round the secluded inlet along a narrow path. Not far past some pleasant picnic spots by the shore (**25min**) the path becomes a track. Shortly, at a signposted junction, keep left to

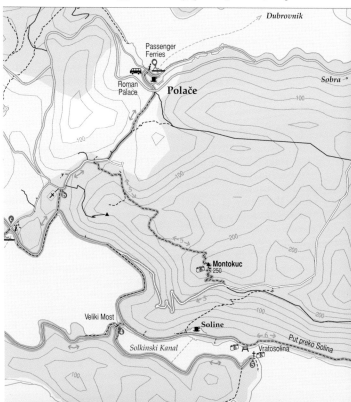

reach **Mali Most** (**❶**; **27min**). Turn right along the road before the bridge. *(But for Shorter walk 1, cross the bridge and return via the eastern and northern shores of the lake; see page 62.)*

To start from Polače, turn right from the jetty (**◐**), then walk up an alley beside the Roman palace (near the archway on the main road). Turn left at a junction and go up a minor road; cross the main road and continue up a stone-paved path, then a wide track/road which you follow across a broad saddle and downhill. Near a cemetery on the right, diverge left down a path (**ⓑ**) to the lakeside road. Turn right to **Pristanište** (**ⓒ**), then left at a road junction. Continue, via the hamlet of **Babine Kuče** (**ⓓ**), to **Mali Most** (**❶**; **1h15min**). Cross the bridge and turn left to follow a road close to the shore. *(But for Shorter walk 1, do not cross the bridge; follow the notes above for the Shorter walk from Pomena, but continue past the turn-off to Pomena, around the lake and back to Mali Most).*

Both versions of the walk now head south on this lakeside road, soon passing a junction on the right and further on, a junction on the left to Villa Jezero, a private residence. Continue to a junction where **Malo Jezero** is nearby to the right, and turn left on a wide track towards VRATOSOLINA (**❷**; **34min/1h22min**). Further on, diverge right along a path sign-posted to ZAKAMENICA (**50min/ 1h45min**). Shortly, bear right, and a superb view of **St Mary's Island** opens up. Gaining height gradually, the path comes to another slightly obscure junction marked by an old post and another fine lookout point (**1h2min/ 1h53min**), where you again bear

right. The path crosses the ridge and descends to **Zakamenica** (**❸**; **1h5min/1h56min**), a spectacular viewpoint, above the waves breaking on the dissected limestone cliffs.

Retrace your steps to the earlier junction where you can turn right towards VRATOSOLINA, down to the lakeside road (**1h15min/2h6min**) *(But for Shorter walk 2 turn left.)* The road meanders east, to a point above another bridge, **Veliki Most** (**❹**; **1h45min/2h36min**; photo page 71), where a side path leads down to the shore of **Veliko Jezero** for a close-up view of the tidal surge through the narrow channel.

Continue along the road, now beside the **Solinski Kanal**, with the hamlet of Soline opposite, through more open ground and past some old olive groves and barriers near the seaward end of the Kanal. Then you pass a tiny sheltered sandy **beach** a short distance from the road's end; from here, follow a path to a **stone cross** (**❺**; **2h15min/3h6min**) above **Vratosolina**, the lakes' outlet. The cross is where Soline fishermen prayed for a safe return; the original is in the church on St Mary's Isle.

To return to Pomena or Polače, retrace steps to **Veliki Most** (**❹**). Cross the bridge and follow the shoreline path to the inlet east of Pristaniste (**2h50min/ 4h5min**). Here, either cross the road and retrace steps to **Polače** (**4h36min**). Or continue along the path to **Pristaniste** (**ⓒ**), then follow the road from there to **Pomena** (**3h55min**). Alternatively, follow a shoreline nature trail from Pristaniste around the Konštar headland to join the road at **Babine Kuče** (add about 5min).

St Mary's Island (Picnic 6)

MLJET NATIONAL PARK

This wonderful national park occupies the northwestern third of the long slender island of Mljet, about 25km northwest of Dubrovnik. It can be visited on a day-long excursion during summer, but is well worth an overnight stay so that you can explore the beautiful lakes and scenic lookouts.

Set aside in 1960, the 3000ha national park protects the beautiful sea lakes, dense Aleppo pine and holm oak forests, 600+ species of Mediterranean vegetation, the rocky coastline and inshore waters; it is a member of the Natura 2000 network of protected areas (see also pages 108 and 160). Its many historic features include the remains of a Roman palace and early Christian basilica at Polače and the 12th-century Benedictine monastery on St Mary's Island. More information is available from the park offices in Pristanište Polače, Pomena and numerous information boards along the walks described.

The car ferry linking Prapratno and Mljet year round is met at Sobra by the local bus which terminates at the small village of Pomena at the western tip of the island. Passenger-only ferries operate between Dubrovnik and Polače and a catamaran service links Spit, Hvar, Korčula, Pomena and Dubrovnik. You need to purchase a park entrance ticket from the park offices at Pomena or Pristanište, or from a kiosk at Polače. It's valid for the duration of your visit and includes one return trip to St Mary's Island (Picnic 6, see page 35); always carry it with you.

Park rules prohibit driving around the lakes within the park, and parking space anywhere is very limited. The three suggested walks in the park (Walks 4-6) include directions from the conveniently located villages of Pomena and Polače, both with a choice of accommodation.

Walk 5 (Mljet): MONTOKUC SUMMIT FROM POMENA OR POLAČE

Distance/time: 10km/6mi; 3h (from Pomena); 5.5km/3.3mi; 2h40min (from Polače).
Grade: ● moderate, with approximately 280m/918ft ascent; on paths, tracks and quiet roads. Signposts and waymarkers
Equipment/map: see page 46; Nakladnik map of Mljet National Park (1:14,000)
Refreshments: available at Pomena, Polače; also at Babine

Kuče on the Pomena route
Transport: 🚢 ferry or catamaran to Mljet (see page 164), then on foot from Pomena or Polače
Nearest accommodation: Pomena, Polače
Shorter walk (from Polače): Montokuc; 4.6km/2.8mi; 2h. ● Moderate, with approximately 320m/1050ft ascent; equipment and transport as above. Retrace steps to Polače from (**❷**).

A̶t 250m, Montokuc's summit is of barely average height by Mljet standards (the highest point reaches 513m in the centre of the island, north of the village of Babino Polje), but it affords a wonderful panorama of distant islands and mountains, and fine local views too.

To start from Pomena, walk from the quay (**○**) to the eastern end of the village, where a **national park sign** points the way up a flight of

stone steps. Follow these up through pines and down to a trail overlooking **Malo Jezero**, then continue left to **Mali Most** (**ⓐ**;

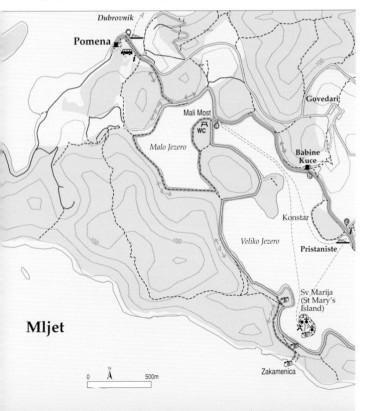

20min). Follow the road along the shore of **Veliko Jezero**, through the hamlet of **Babine Kuče** (ⓑ). Pass above a shallow valley planted with vines to arrive at **Pristanište** (ⓐ; **30min**).

Rather than keeping to the road, from beside the national park's direction signs start descending steps towards the shore, then bear left and follow a path down to the water's edge. The path skirts a minor cliff, passes below a curious boomerang-shaped monument, then generally parallels the shore to the head of a small **inlet** (ⓒ; **45min**).

Go up steps to the road, cross to a park direction sign to Polače, and continue up a wide clear trail. Turn right at a road and walk up to a junction with a path on the right where there's a **sign** to MONTOKUC (❶; **50min**).

To start from Polače, turn right from the jetty (◐), then walk up an alley beside the Roman palace (near the archway on the main road). Turn left at a junction and go up a minor road; cross the main road and continue up a stone-paved path, then a wide track/road across a broad saddle, to the signposted turn-off to MONTOKUC (❶; **25min**).

Both versions of the walk now continue along the path, gaining height steadily through pine woodland. Turn sharp right towards MONTOKUC as indicated (**1h10min/45min**). Continue up to the rocky summit of **Montokuc** (❷; **1h30min/1h5min**), where there are a fire watcher's lookout and two park information boards. The view embraces the Pelješac peninsula and Svete Ilija (Walk 7) to the north, the low dark profile

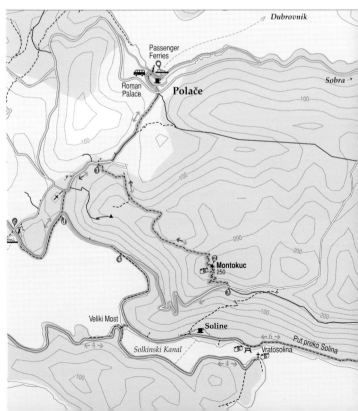

of the island of Korčula to the northwest and Lastovo, far out to sea in the west. *(For the Shorter walk, simply retrace your steps from here to Polače.)*

To continue on the main, circular route, face the national park's signboards and bear right, downhill, on a clear waymarked path. It bears left and zigzags down through forest. On meeting a **track** (**❸**), turn right and continue down to the road beside **Veliko Jezero** (**❹**; **2h10min/1h45min**).

To return to Pomena, continue along the path below the road to **Pristanište** (**ⓐ**; **2h25min**); bear left here and walk via **Babine Kuče** (**ⓑ**), **Mali Most** (**ⓒ** and **Malo Jezero** to the steps leading up and over to **Pomena** (**3h**).

To return to Polače, follow the road back to the unmarked Polače turn-off at the head of a small **inlet** (**ⓓ**) and from there follow the path, then road and tracks, up and over and back to **Polače** (**2h40min**).

Fire watch and viewpoint on the rocky summit of Montokuc

Walk 6 (Mljet): SOLINE FROM POMENA OR POLAČE

Distance/time: 13.5km/8.1mi; 3h20min from Pomena; 11.4km/7mi; 2h50min from Polače
Grade: ● easy-moderate (90m/295ft ascent from Pomena, 170m/558ft ascent from Polače). On paths, quiet roads and tracks, well signposted
Equipment/map: see page 46; walking shoes suitable; swimming things; Nakladnik map of Mljet National Park (1:14,000)
Refreshments: available at Pomena, Polače, Soline; also at Babine Kuče on the Pomena route
Transport: ⛴ ferry or catamaran to Mljet (see page 164), then on foot from Pomena or Polače
Nearest accommodation: Pomena, Polače

If the wind is blowing strongly from the southeast, the turbulent seas crashing onto the south coast contrast excitingly with the tranquillity of the lakes. Soline, a hamlet founded in 1825 as a fishing settlement, owes its name to the production of salt there by the Benedictine monks from St Mary's Island. The nearby barriers across the channel are intended to limit the flow of marine debris into the lakes.

To start from Pomena, follow the notes for Walk 5 on page 66 to the head of the small **inlet** at **Veliko Jezero** (❶; **45min**, ❻ on Walk 5).

To start from Polače, turn right from the jetty (○), then walk up an alley beside the Roman palace (near the archway on the main road). Turn left at a junction and go up a minor road; cross the main road and continue up a stone-paved path, then a wide track/road across a broad saddle, to the signposted turn-off to *MONTOKUC* (❻; **25min**; Walk 5). Leave the road near a cemetery on the right, taking a path down to the road beside **Veliko Jezero** (❶; **35min**).

Both versions of the walk continue from here. Rather than walk along the road, drop down towards the shore of the lake, bear left along a stone-built boat landing, and follow a narrow path to **Veliki Most** (❷; **1h10min/1h**) for a close-up view of the tidal surge through the narrow channel. The channel was bridged until 1960, when it was enlarged at the behest of Marshal Tito to allow the passage of wider boats. The bridge has been replaced with an elegant, high-arched, skilfully built structure (see panel overleaf).

From here retreat to the road and follow it to the hamlet of **Soline** (❸; **1h18min/1h8min**). *(For a shorter walk, retrace steps to your starting point from here.)*

But for dramatic sea vistas, continue along the road for about 400m, to its end. There's a national park sign here, *PUT PREKO SOLINA*. Follow this path through pines; it fades across open rocky ground above **Vratosolina** (❹), the outer limit of the channel linking the lakes to the sea. Here you'll find some picnic tables.

The path continues generally eastwards to a deep inlet called **Grabova** (about 2km return). However the pine woodland through which it passes is strewn with grey fallen trees and branches making it somewhat less than attractive. The above distances and times are to/from this inlet, from where you retrace steps. But you may choose to turn back from Vratsolina.

JOSIP BROZ TITO

'Our Tito' as he has been wryly called, makes five appearances in this book, directly in the Mljet and Paklenica national parks and on the island of Vis, and indirectly on the islands of Goli Otok and Grgur between Rab and Krk.

Tito was Yugoslavia's Marshal and President for life from 1949 until his death in 1980. Born Josip Broz in 1892, he assumed the name Tito, after the 18th-century Croatian writer Tito Brezovački, as he rose rapidly through the Yugoslav Communist Party ranks during the 1930s. He is probably best remembered as the leader of the Partisans during World War II, for standing up to Stalin in defence of his own brand of pink Yugosavian Communism, and as a co-founder of the still-functioning non-aligned group of nations.

At home there was a darker side to his reputation. Despite his avowed commitment to promotion of the common rather than individual good, he lived lavishly. He ordered the channel between the two lakes in Mljet National Park to be widened to allow luxury cruisers to pass through. As an absolute dictator, he neither tolerated ethnic conflict, nor brooked dissent. Goli Otok was turned into an appalling gulag for dissenters; nearby Grgur was a women's prison.

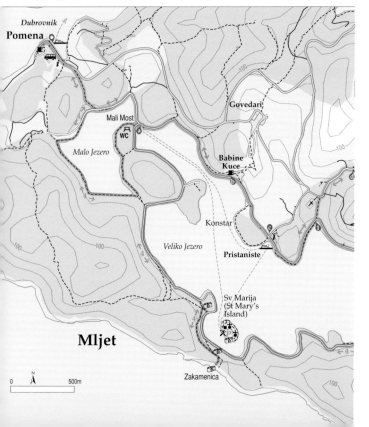

Veliki Most

Though his death was widely mourned, he fell far out of favour in the early years of Croatia's independence. However, as older Croatians recalled the standard of living they enjoyed during the 1970s, he eventually emerged from the cold for at least some people.

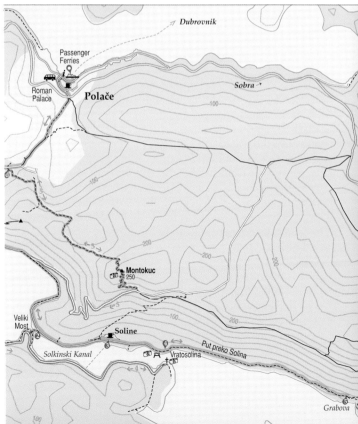

Walk 7 (Pelješac peninsula): SVETE ILIJA SUMMIT FROM OREBIĆ

Distance/time: 16.8km/10.4mi; 6h30min
Grade: ● strenuous, with approximately 970m/3182ft ascent. On paths and quiet roads, almost all well waymarked
Equipment/map: see page 46; walking poles; Geodetski map of Pelješac Riviera (1:25,000)
Refreshments: only in Orebić
Transport: 🚌 from Dubrovnik or 🚗 car or ⛴ passenger ferry from Korčula town to Orebić (see Transport, page 164). Park by the ferries (42° 58.476'N, 17° 10.497'E)
Nearest accommodation: Orebić, Korčula town

Shorter walks

1 Franciscan monastery; 3km/ 1.8mi; 1h10min. Easy, with 155m/508ft ascent; walking shoes suitable; transport as for the main walk. Follow the main walk to ❸ for views of Korčula; return by the same route.

2 Viewpoint; 9km/5.4mi; 3h20min. Moderate, with approximately 520m/1706ft ascent; equipment and transport as for the main walk. Follow the main walk to ❺ for marvellous wide views; return by the same route.

3 Franciscan monastery — viewpoint; 6km/3.6mi; 2h10min. ● Easy-moderate, with approximately 365m/1197ft ascent; equipment as for the main walk. Transport by 🚌: from the junction of the main and shoreside roads at the western end of Orebić, drive west towards Viganje/Lovište for 0.4km, then turn right up a road signposted BILOPOLJE, to a small car park on the western side of the monastery (42° 58.659'N, 17° 9.140'E). Follow the main walk from ❸ to the **viewpoint** (❺) at the 1h30min-mark for the fine views; return by the same route.

4 Franciscan monastery — Svete Ilija; 13.4km/8.3mi; 5h20min. ● Strenuous, with 815m/2649ft ascent; equipment as for the main walk; transport as for Shorter walk 3 above. Follow the main walk from the monastery (❸) and back.

The Pelješac peninsula between Dubrovnik and Makarska is a spectacularly rugged finger of rocky mountainscapes, a region of striking contrasts where much of the flat land between the soaring peaks is planted with vineyards and olive groves. Svete Ilija (961m/3152ft), a rugged massif near its western extremity and the objective of this rewarding walk, dominates the peninsula and is visible from afar. En route to Orebić, it struck me that with a slight rise in sea level, Pelješac would become an island, elevating Svete Ilija to the status of highest peak in the Adriatic islands.

The small town of Orebić at the foot of the massif is the convenient base from which to tackle the ascent. Alternatively, the lovely old town of Korčula, sometimes called 'mini Dubrovnik', is only a short ferry trip away.

Start the walk at the more westerly of the two car parks near the ferry terminals by following the promenade (**O**). About 50m past Hotel Indijan turn right up a lane (Setalište Skvar); skirt a vacant plot then go left at the main road. Continue for about 150m, to a point opposite the Bellevue hotel's **tennis courts** on the left. From here take the **unmarked path** (**❶**) on the right, up into the pine forest. Shortly, cross a road and continue on a wide, well way-marked path signposted to FRANJE-VACKI SAMOSTAN. The gradient steepens then the path swings right and rises to a road (**❷**; **30min**).

Turn left and follow the road past a large **cemetery**, the dour **Franciscan monastery** and the adjacent church of **Our Lady of the Angels** (with car park; **❸**; **35min**; Picnic 7). *(Shorter walk 1 returns direct from here; Shorter walks 3 and 4 start here.)* The view across to Korčula town is very fine, with Mljet island beyond to the southeast.

Continue along the road, bearing left at a junction, to a fork in the hamlet of **Bilopolje** (**❹**; **45min**). Turn right on the track signposted to SVETE ILIJA, beside information about an Educational Trail and Advice to Walkers. Very shortly, go left in front of a house to a junction where you turn steeply up to the right. In a few minutes you emerge from the trees, as the path rises across the steep slope. The spring wildflowers almost everywhere are marvellous: sage, beautiful blue irises, pink cistus and many more. At the end of a gravelly stretch the view westwards begins to unfold, then opens out further on at a **viewpoint** (**❺**; **1h40min**), revealing the islands of Korčula, Vis (out to

On the Svete Ilija ridge

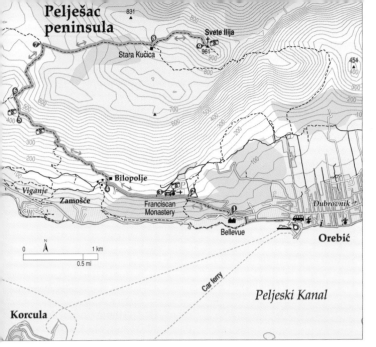

sea) and slender Hvar. *(Shorter walks 2 and 3 return direct from here.)*

There follows a marked changed of direction (**1h50min**), as the path bends right (northeast) above a deep valley, to traverse its flank — there's some welcome shade along here. Pass a way-marked junction to KUCISTE on the coast (**6**; **2h**). The path crosses the top of the valley, then rises to cross a spur. At a signposted fork, bear right (east) towards SV ILIJA (**7**; **2h30min**), through pine woodland where there are information boards about mouflon (wild sheep), wildflowers and karst formations (see opposite).

The character of the woodland soon changes, then the gradient steepens and you reach a small stone building called '**Stara Kučica**' (**8**; **3h**); continue up behind it past a signposted path for an alternative route back to Orebić. Bear right across open

ground and climb gently to tackle the summit ridge. The path dips and twists through the maze of weirdly sculpted boulders — a typical karst formation — up to the summit of **Svete Ilija** (**9**; **3h30min**) with a cross and granite plaque confirming that you're in the right place. In the cairn beneath the cross is a metal box containing a visitors' book. The magnificent panoramic view takes in several islands, the coastal mountain ranges and the rugged Pelješac peninsula, but neither Orebić nor Korčula town.

The descent is straightforward, retracing your steps: back to **Stara Kučica** (**8**), down to the road at **Bilopolje** (**4**; **5h50min**) and on to the **monastery** (**3**). Five minutes further down, about 60m past two houses on the left, leave the road at **2**: go right down a path and follow it to the Viganje road; turn left and continue into **Orebić** (**6h30min**).

KARST LANDSCAPES

It's next to impossible to get away from limestone in the Adriatic islands and coastal mountains. You can find conglomerate outcrops, but the tough sedimentary rock and its close relative, dolomite, dominate the landscape — dazzling white in the Krk uplands, smoky grey on the Paklenica cliffs.

Many paths across plateaus and along ridge crests weave through intricate mazes of deeply dissected, sharp-edged limestone — one of the features of the geological formation known as karst.

Essentially, it's the result of absorption of water by porous surface limestone and the widening of lines of weakness in the rock. Water percolates further down, eventually creating underground rivers and caves; thus, the virtual absence of surface water is a characteristic of karst landscapes.

Caves can — well, cave in, and soil accumulates in the resulting surface depression. In the past these precious areas of cultivable ground, known as *poljes*, were enclosed by stone walls, creating green islands, transformed to lakes after heavy rain. They're still much in evidence, as you'll see on many walks, such as Svete Ilija (Walk 7) and Hlam (Walk 31 on page 145).

Classic karst formations in the Paklenica National Park (Short picnic walk 20)

MAKARSKA RIVIERA: **Introduction**

The Makarska Riviera, the rugged 60km-long section of coast between Gradac in the east and Brela westwards, centering on the eponymous resort town, may not seem like an attractive venue for walkers. However, on the two headlands guarding Makarska's harbour, the coastline, and the foothills of the mighty Biokovo range, you'll find peaceful secluded coves and woodlands, superb coast and mountain views and a fascinating botanical garden. The seemingly inexorable proliferation of apartment blocks and commercial buildings has compromised some traditional routes between once-isolated villages, but all is not lost ! Short walks on the surprisingly natural wooded headlands introduce scenery typical all along the coast: low cliffs, inlets and beaches (some with the treasured Blue Flag designation), between Makarska and Luka. The Biokovo range is protected by its namesake Natural Park; its towering, seemingly impenetrable cliffs accessible via a skilfully built path. The botanical garden presents an unusual opportunity to learn about the flora and fauna of the cliffs, screes and hardy woodlands of the slopes.

Any of the coastal towns and villages can be the base for all six of the walks covered here. There's a regular local bus service along the coast road and long distance routes connect Makarska to destinations throughout the country. Ferries ply between Sumartin on Brač and Makarska.

For more information go to www.makarskainfo.com.

Photo: Plaža Nugal below the Biokovo range, near Makarska (Short 'picnic' walk 9)

Walk 8 (Makarska Riviera): FROM MAKARSKA TO BAŠKA VODA

Nearby setting shown opposite
Distance/time: 10km/6mi; 2h20min
Grade: ● easy, with 25m/82ft ascent; on paths, tracks, quiet roads
Equipment/map: see page 46; walking shoes or trekking sandals suitable; SMAND map 32: Biokovo (1:25,000)
Refreshments: available at small towns and villages along the route
Transport: 🚗 or 🚌 to Makarska; return on local 🚌 from Baška Voda: the stop (⑥) is on the seafront road near the southern end of the harbour and indicated by a bus logo sign. Or return by

one of the fairly frequent intercity 🚌 services: walk up the road signposted to Dubrovnik. At a T-junction turn right (12min), then almost immediately left, up Ulica Ivana Mestrovica. This leads to the highway; the bus stop (⑦) is 30m to the right. (See Transport, page 164.)
Nearest accommodation: Makarska, Baška Voda
Shorter walk: Krvavica 8.6km/ 5.2mi; 2h32min. ● Easy; equipment as for main walk. Transport: 🚗 or 🚌 to Makarska. Follow the main walk to ❷, then retrace steps.
Alternative: See notes on page 78.

For a popular, well-developed area, the Makarska Riviera, northwards from the town, offers walks through remarkably secluded woodland and along the coast, interspersed with harbours, quiet coves, waterside cafés and bars. Views of the Biokovo mountains, the islands, and locally along the indented rocky shore are a constant delight. To continue this walk northwestwards, see Walk 9 overleaf.

Start the walk from the western end of **Makarska harbour** near Hotel Miramare: follow a path to the right through wooded parkland. Join the **promenade** (Put Cvitaćke), running the gauntlet of innumerable stalls, then a string of bars and cafés. Past a tiny bay between two slender fingers of shingle, the path leads on in and out of pine woods and olive groves and on to a **shingle beach** (❶; **55min**) and a magnificent view of the Biokovo mountains; Makarska could be a million miles away.

Continue through pines, where there are signs of much older settlement: stone walls, mounds of stones and terraces. From the far end of a small cove (**1h5min**) an amazing path snakes along the base of crumbling cliffs just above high tide level. When the path ends,

cross shingle to a paved path through pines. Pass a deserted hotel, then follow a road briefly to **Kravica** and its small harbour (❷; **1h25min**). (*The Shorter walk returns from here.*) Go up a road overlooking a boatyard to another road. This takes you back to the shore and shingle beach at the tranquil village of **Bratuš** (❸; **1h37min**). Continue along the promenade, with houses on the right. Then, with houses on both sides, join Put Makarkse and descend to **Promajna** (❹; **1h46min**), where there's a small supermarket and a shingle beach.

Follow the roadside path, then the edge of the road (Ulica Obala); it soon bends left and you join a path. Continue through olive groves above a shingle beach, then pine woodlands, past a sign

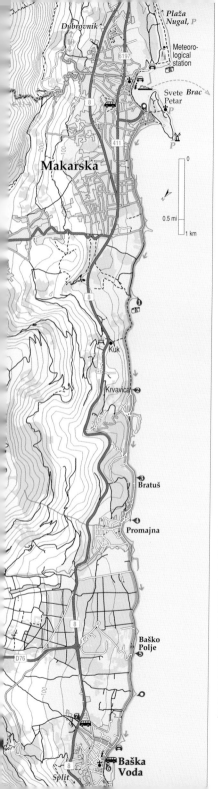

welcoming pets to a nearby beach, to the village of **Baško Polje** (**⑤**; **2h7min**). A narrow path on the left leads on across open ground. Beyond a small **sculpture** on the right commemorating the navy landing preceding the liberation of Baška Voda during WWII, descend to a sea level path which takes you around **Plaža Nikolina, a Blue Flag beach**, to the centre of **Baška Voda** (**2h20min**).

Alternative: You can do this walk in reverse from **Baška Voda** (for Transport see page 164). Follow the roadside path along the shore, then a minor road above a shingle beach. From open ground (**5min**) there's a fine view of Vošac (Walk 11). A path leads on beyond apartments through pines beside a **shingle beach** (**16min**). A few minutes further on, go up steps, to bypass a building on the right, then return to the shore. Reaching **Promajna** (**④**; **45min**), walk along a road then a roadside path. From the post office at the far end of the bay, bear left up a minor road sign-posted to *MAKARSKA*, shortly keeping right. The path becomes a narrow clifftop road. Descend to the promenade beside the shingle beach at **Bratuš** (**③**). From there a road takes you up to the clifftop (**1h7min**). Soon, descend steeply to a boatyard at **Krvavica** (**②**). Continue parallel with the shore, across **shingle** (**①**; **1h18min**), to the path along the base of the colourful cliffs. Walk on through pines and bear left through a gap in a stone wall (**1h34min**). The track leads in and out of pines and Svete Petar at Makarska comes into view briefly (**1h52min**). Paths and tracks lead on to the outskirts of Makarska. Near the far end of the beach, keep right past refreshment stalls, then bend left by a disco, to **Makarska harbour** (**2h20min**).

Walk 9 (Makarska Riviera): FROM BAŠKA VODA TO UVALA LUKA AND RETURN

See also photo page 2
Distance/time: 12km/7.2mi; 2h48min
Grade: ● easy; on paved paths and shingle briefly
Equipment/map: see page 46; walking shoes or trekking sandals are suitable; SMAND map 32: Biokovo (1:25,000)
Refreshments: available at each small town/village along the way.
Transport: 🚌 from Makarska (see Transport, page 164) or 🚤 to Baška Voda: from Makarska take the E65; the turn-off to Baška is clearly signposted (7km); after 0.6km bear left. There is a large car park at the western end of the harbour (43° 21.535'N, 16° 56.722'E).
Nearest accommodation: Makarska, Baška Voda
Shorter walk: Punta Rata; 6km/ 3.6mi; 1h30min. ● Easy; equipment, transport as for the main walk. Follow the main walk to ❷ and retrace steps.

Despite the fact that the Makarska Riviera is, in places, an over-developed seaside resort, it's still not difficult to reach more or less natural, peaceful countryside. A shoreside path, skilfully landscaped with seats and trees, leads to the tranquil hamlet of Luka, tucked into a small bay overlooked by a steep, wooded mountainside. En route you pass Plaža Berulia and Punta Rata, two of Croatia's many Blue Flag beaches (119 in 2019) — those which have met strict, internationally-recognised criteria for pollution, water quality, environmental management and education, and safety and services.

Start out from **Baška Voda** by walking along the **promenade** (**O**) between the shorefront road and the shingle beach, past the **harbour**. As the promenade starts to rise go left down steps to a path beside the shingle and on to **Punta Rata beach**. At the far end climb steps to a path, then shortly descend to the promenade in the small town of **Brela** (**❶**). Go on to another shingle beach at **Punta**

79

Rata itself (**❷**; **45min**). *(The Shorter walk returns from here.)*

A wide path leads on beside the shore, well away from the nearest road. Soon you come to the **Rock of Brela** (**❸**; **51min**), a massive boulder moored just offshore. Once home to monk seals, the rock became famous in the heyday of postcards as the symbol of that town. A little further on there's a similar, more complex but less attractive formation.

Continue past the hamlet of **Podrace** (**❹**) and around **Rt Šćit** (**❺**; **1h3min**). The coast is now much quieter, with fewer bars and souvenir shops, and cliffs excluding buildings from the shoreline. Almost immediately you reach **Uvala Stomarica**, where a few of the houses even have gardens.

It's another 14 minutes to **Uvala Poderblaje** (**❻**). Beyond the next headland, the formal path ends at the shallow bay of **Uvala Luka** (**❼**; **1h24min**), where there's a café or two and a convenient seat at the far end.

To return to **Baška Voda** simply retrace your steps — the views are always quite different from the opposite direction (**2h48min**).

Rock of Brela, near Punta Rata

Walk 10 (Makarska Riviera): BIOKOVO BOTANIC GARDEN FROM MAKARSKA

See also photo on page 86
Distance/time: 13km/7.8mi;
about 2h30min from Makarska
Grade: ● moderate, with
450m/1479ft ascent; on quiet
roads, unsurfaced roads, tracks,
paths. Signposted; waymarking to
the Makar–Mlinice junction
Equipment/map: see page 46;
walking poles; SMAND map 32:
Biokovo (1:25,000)
Refreshments: available only in
Makarska
Transport: 🚌 or 🚐 to Makarska;
🚌 to Kotišina (optional)
Nearest accommodation:
Makarska

Shorter walk: Biokovo Botanic
Garden from Kotišina; 3km/
1.8mi. ● Easy-moderate, with
approximately 100m/330ft ascent;
allow at least an hour. Equipment
as for main walk. Access by 🚌:
from the centre of Makarska drive
southeast along either route 6197
or route 8 and turn left at a
junction by a large Konzum
supermarket along route 512 for
VRGORAK. Continue for under 1km
to a junction signposted to
KOTISINA. There is limited parking
space at waypoint ❹ (the 1h30min
mark of the main walk; 43° 17.369'N,
17° 2.722'E).

Biokovo Nature Park extends northeast along the range
from above the town of Podgora south of Makarska to
just beyond the hamlet of Luka (Walk 9). The park protects
a remarkable variety of
plants, from Mediterranean
to alpine species, small
herds of chamois and
mouflon (wild sheep) and
extensive outcrops of karst
limestone features. The
range reaches its highest
point at Svete Jure
(1762m) and there are 14
peaks in all above 1400m.
In the foothills, between
350m and 500m, is Bio-
kovo Botanical Garden (as
part of the wider Nature
Park), set aside in 1981,
thanks to the dedicated
efforts of Franciscan priest
and scholar Dr Fra Jure
Radic (1920-1990). The
garden's mission is scien-
tific research, protection
and conservation of Bio-
kovo's native flora. Within
its 16.5ha, the flora and

81

The medieval castle in Biokovo Nature Park

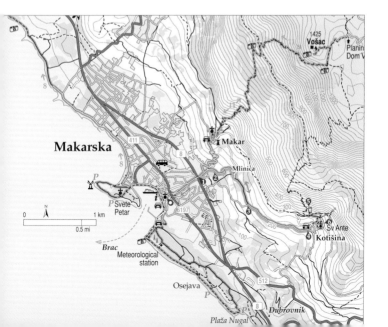

wildlife of the screes, crags and of Proslap Kanyon are presented in near-natural settings. There's also the substantial remnant of a 17th-century castle, almost literally pasted onto the cliffs, and a 17th-century church. There's much more information at https://pp-biokovo.hr/en.

Start the walk at **Trg Fra Andrije Kačića Mosica** (**0**), with the statue of the eponymous priest in front of the imposing 18th-century **Church of Svete Marko** shown on page 86. Walk up its left hand side to Ulica Don Mihovila Pavlinoviča. Cross this road diagonally left and almost immediately turn right. Walk up the steep waymarked lane and across the **highway overpass** (**1**).

Continue straight uphill for 100m to a junction where Makar is to the left and almost immediately turn right towards *MLINICE* (**20min**). The road (Put Mlinica) dips across a **small valley** (**2**; **30min**) then bends left into another one and climbs steeply. Beyond a right bend the road crosses a stream; shortly, at a junction, turn right for *KOTISINA* on an unsurfaced road. Then, at a **T-junction** (**3**), go left along a road for the *BOTANIC GARDEN*. As you round a bend, a wide valley fills the view (**1h**).

About 100m beyond **house no 10** on your right, where a sign says it's 600m to the *GARDEN*, look up to the left for the first sighting of the old castle built against the cliffs. Then, just past a WWII memorial, go left with a *GARDEN* sign (**4**; **1h30min**). Motorists should be able to tuck in somewhere here for the Shorter walk. Nearby is an information board outlining the life and work of **Fr Jure Radic**, founder of the Biokovo Nature Park.

Continue up to a junction

where you go straight on for *BIOKOVO BOTANIC GARDEN*. Just ahead is the start of the main path, skilfully built across the rocky terrain, with benches here and there. There are a few notices about endemic plants and other topics. I haven't given any precise times for an exploration as there's so much to see, so the following notes describe just one possible route.

Shortly, at another junction, turn left for the *GARDEN* and you come to the main entrance. Nearby a short path leads to the remarkable 17th-century **castle** (**5**), so built as to be almost indistinguishable from the cliff face. Further on you may notice a sign on the left to *KANYON PROSLAP*, a seasonal waterfall, but the path is steep and involves some minor scrambling. Beyond this go down a rather stony path towards *MAKIJA* and you come to a road. **Svete Ante church** (**6**) is nearby to the left. At time of writing an archaeological dig was underway inside the church, in search of the remains of the original church on which it was built. On-site information will be installed once it's complete.

Follow a sign to the *ENTRY* to reach the access road in seven minutes. From here simply retrace your steps to Makarska; allow 15 minutes to a junction to Makar on the right, another 25 minutes to Put Makar and 20 minutes down to the start — an hour in all, for a total walking time of **2h30min**.

Walk 11 (Makarska Riviera): VOŠAC VIEWPOINT FROM MAKARSKA

Distance/time: 8km/5mi; 4h30min from Makarska
Grade: ● moderate, with 800m/ 2624ft ascent; on quiet suburban and rural roads, well-waymarked paths
Equipment: see page 46; walking poles for the descent; SMAND map 32: Biokovo (1:25,000)
Refreshments: available only in Makarska
Transport: 🚗 or 🚐 to/from Makarska (see pages 164-165)
Nearest accommodation: Makarska
Shorter walk: Viewpoint from Makar; 3.4km/2mi; 2h30min. ● Moderate, with 600m/1968ft

ascent; equipment as for main walk. Transport by 🚗: from the southern junction of the A8 and the 6197 road to Makarska centre, drive north along the A8 for 2km to a slip road on the left signed to Makar. Go right at once, over the highway and up the steep road to Makar; there's space for a few cars opposite the cemetery (43° 18.006'N, 17° 1.705'E). Join the walk here at ❷.
Alternative walk: Vošac summit; 10km/6mi; 7h30min. ● Very strenuous, with 1225m/4018ft of ascent/descent. Access and equipment as above. Follow the main walk to the viewpoint at ❹, then pick up the notes on page 85.

Vošac (1425m/4674ft) isn't the highest peak in the Biokovo range (that honour belongs to Svete Jure, 1762m, further north), but it dominates the town of Makarska sprawling at its foot. Gazing up towards its summit, you

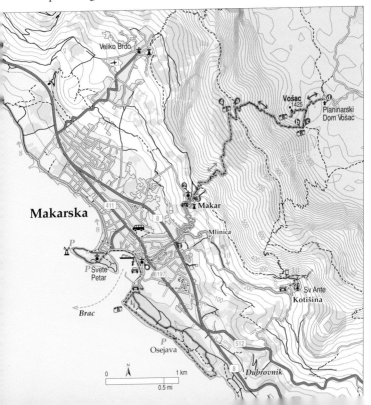

simply would not believe that it's possible to broach even the lower slopes, let alone reach that exalted point without the help of metal steps and chains. Instead, a superbly designed and built path, rarely steep, winds up the severely steep slope from the village of Makar, exploiting wooded ground and gravelly gaps wherever possible, and providing a veritable bird's-eye view of the town, the coast and islands. This walk provides an excellent introduction to the range which is also the venue for Walk 10 on pages 81-83). Along the way, you may be lucky enough to spot a chamois, a rare experience in Croatia except in high mountain areas(see page 81).

Start the walk at **Trg Fra Andrije Kačića Mosica** (**O**), with the statue of the eponymous priest in front of the imposing 18th-century **Church of Svete Marko** shown on page 86. Walk up its left hand side to Ulica Don Mihovila Pavlinoviča. Cross this road diagonally left and almost immediately turn right. Walk up the steep waymarked lane and across the **highway overpass** (**❶**). Continue straight uphill for 100m, then go left for *MAKAR*, still on the very steep lane. Go round a right bend past house 91 on the left, always following the waymarkers. The road zigzags up to the village of **Makar** (**❷**; **45min**). *(The Shorter walk starts here.)* Opposite the small church is a large Biokovo Nature Park information board which contains two photos of Makarska , one from 1933, the other from 2017; you wonder whether this is the same place!

Bear right opposite the **cemetery and church** and follow the road round, past a **memorial** on the right, then bear left at a minor junction. A few steps further on, take a path on the right with red pointers to 'VOŠAC 3H' and 'SV JURE 5H' (**❸**). Walk up, soon passing a house on the left; bear left and go up behind the house. The path winds up to a

small level area, where you continue straight up into pine woodland. Emerging from the woods (**1h20min**) the path carves a series of long zigzags across the steep slope; then, at a left bend, turns into a **shallow valley** (**1h30min**). Pause along here and look up — you can see the blunt triangle of Vošac's summit not too far above. With the gradient easing slightly, the path enters a shady stretch in the middle of which is a pleasant **grassy clearing** (**2h5min**). A few minutes later, you're back in the open, drawing level with the top of a spur on the left, a fine **viewpoint** (**❹**; **2h15min**). From here retrace your steps to Makar, if you parked there (**3h45min**) or to **Makarska** (**4h30min**). *(But for the Alternative walk to the summit carry on from here.)*

Alternative walk
Beyond a knot of zigzags, pass a junction on the left (**❺**; to Veliko Brdo; **2h5min**). You'll notice that the pines have virtually disappeared, giving way to birch and juniper. From a **small flat area** close to the foot of the vertical cliffs (**2h50min**) the path leads up to a **distinct gap** (**3h25min**) between the cliffs and a big bluff on the right. Then it's a comparatively easy pull up to the main

ridge and a **viewpoint** enclosed by a low wall (**ⓑ**; **3h45min**). Ignore the waymarked path eastwards to 'Kotišina' from here (**❹**).

To reach the summit, follow a waymarked path towards the peak crowned by a tall tower — Svete Jure (1762m), Biokovo's highest. At a junction (**3h55min**) bear left up a waymarked path. (The path to the right leads to **ⓒ**, Planinarski Dom Vošac, a mountain hut where refreshments may be available in peak season.) Climb easily enough to the broad summit of **Vošac** (**ⓓ**; **4h20min**). The stone building here, once an army outpost, is now used by the local mountaineering club. The view embraces most of the island of Brač, serpentine Hvar, Korčula, vast mountain ranges to the north and south, and the string of coastal towns.

For the descent retrace your steps via the Kotišina (**ⓒ**) and Veliko Brdo (**ⓐ**) junctions and **Makar** (**❷**) to **Makarska** (**7h30min**).

The walk begins here, at the 18th-century cathedral church of Svete Marko

BRAC: *Introduction*

Brač is probably best known for its beautiful sandy beach, Zlatni Rat (Golden Point), just west of the small town of Bol. But of course there's much more to this, the third largest island in the Adriatic. It rises precipitously from its southern coast to Vidova Gora, at 780m the highest summit along that coast. It crowns the surrounding karst limestone plateau, typical of the island's higher reaches, as is the Aleppo pine and holm oak woodland clustered in sheltered, steep-sided valleys. The island's long history began in prehistoric times; it was ruled by Romans, Venetians, was part of the Austro-Hungarian empire and was occupied only briefly, by Italian forces, during World War II. Spanning these centuries are the many Christian churches, large and small. Wine production has an ancient lineage and is currently thriving, using Plavac mali grapes to produce a rich red.

The three walks described here are based at Bol, crouched at the foot of Vidova Gora, its old heart a fascinating maze of narrow streets, and the whole with a keen feeling of remoteness, at the end of a spectacular winding road. By following part or all of these walks you will find examples of these landscapes and historic features: on the climb of Vidova Gora; on a journey to isolated Blaca monastery and an exploration of the cultivated hillsides east of the town. Brač is linked by catamarans and car ferries to the mainland and to other islands in the southern Adriatic; Bol is adequately served by the island's bus service.

Photo: Zlatni Rat

Walk 12 (Brač): FROM BOL TO SVETE LUCIJA AND GORNJE SMOKOVJE

Distance/time: 4.8km/2.9mi; 2h30min
Grade: ● easy, with approximately 240m/787ft ascent; on quiet roads and tracks
Equipment/map: see page 46; Bol Tourist Board trekking leaflet (approximately 1:25,000)
Refreshments: only in Bol
Transport: 🚌 or 🚢 to Bol (see Transport, page 165). Car parking space is limited: park along the seafront, at the eastern end of the harbour (43° 15.690'N, 16° 39.490'E), or near the bus stop on Obala Vladimira Nazora at the western end (43° 15.627'N, 16° 39.291'E); there are also two large car parks on the western edge of the town.
Nearest accommodation: Bol

Eastwards from Bol, the broad apron of stony ground between the long line of cliffs and the shore is easily accessible on foot. Here the landscape of terraces and fields enclosed by stone walls has probably changed little for a century or more, though fewer terraces are now cultivated. This walk, therefore, takes a step back in time to the days when motorised access was unknown.

Start the walk along the **promenade in Bol** (**O**): walk east, past the past the catamaran terminal and up left along the promenade called Račić which becomes Ulica Ante Stančevića. At a fork bear right then almost beside a playground go left up steps, past an 18th-century windmill and turn right along Šetalište Anđelka Rabadana, soon passing a derelict building with a colourful mural on its gable end and graffiti elsewhere. Turn left up Ulica Tina Ujevića, where the 15th-century **Dominican monastery and museum** (**❶**) and the **oldest church in Bol** from the 9th or 10th century are to the right.

When you reach a junction, turn right along what soon becomes a **track** (**❷**; **20min**). As you gain a little height between scattered houses and olive groves, look out for a good view of the monastery.

You pass tiny **Svete Lucija chapel**, dating from the 18th century (**❸**; **30min**). Stay on the track, traversing gently up the steep slope above old terraces, with beautiful views of the island of Hvar. Shortly, at a fork, keep left on the track, gaining height (**❹**; **45min**). When you come to a junction with signposts for *HIKING TRAIL* and *BICYCLE PATH*, stay on the latter; the former fades into dense

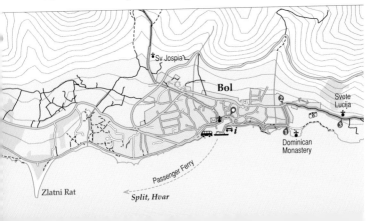

Dominican monastery at Bol

vegetation. The track crosses a small valley (**Dornje Smokovje**) with a few buildings on the seaward slope. The next similarly signposted junction is more helpful — continue straight on (bike route 767) past young vines clinging to the steep hillside. Soon the precipitous cliffs above **Gornje Smokovje** appear (**1h17min**). This wide terraced valley, dotted with huge mounds of stones

painstakingly gathered to make the ground cultivatable, shelters small vineyards and stone buildings — a good place for a break. (The track continues to Gornje Humac (refreshments) at an elevation of 450m and 13km in all from Bol. There you could catch a bus on the Bol–Supetar route back down to Bol (see Transport, page 165).

But this walk turns back from here to **Bol** (**2h30min**).

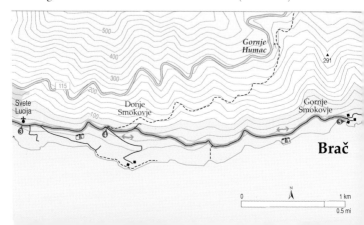

Walk 13 (Brač): VIDOVA GORA SUMMIT FROM BOL

Distance/time: 14km/8.4mi; 4h30min

Grade: ● moderate, with 780m/ 2558ft ascent. On quiet roads and paths; a few signposts and way-marking from the 15min-mark

Equipment/map: see page 46; walking poles for the descent; Bol Tourist Board trekking leaflet

(approximately 1:25,000)

Refreshments: available only in Bol

Transport: 🚐 or 🚢 to Bol (see Transport, page 165, and notes on page 88 about parking)

Nearest accommodation: Bol

Short walk: see Picnic 10, page 36.

At 780m (2558ft), Vidova Gora is the highest peak in the Adriatic islands. It towers above the attractive, small town of Bol on Brač's south coast, its huge grey limestone bluffs and cliffs seemingly inaccessible to walkers. Yet a skilfully built path finds a way up a series of small valleys below its eastern ramparts, so well designed that steep stretches are rare. A path to delight the senses, it passes through pine wood, and its lower reaches are lined with aro-matic, spring-flowering rosemary; it's even well shaded on the whole. The view from the top sweeps round from the Pelješac peninsula and Korčula in the south, past Vis and

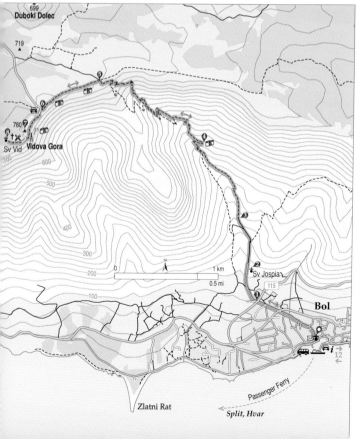

Hvar — where Sv Nikola (Walk 17, page 101, is discernible — to take in the Biokovo range and Makarska to the north, and of course, Bol and Zlatni Rat beach below, one of Croatia's many Blue Flag beaches.

Start out at **Bol Harbour:** walk up the wide street (**O**) with **Gospe ad Karmela church** on the right and the **post office** on the left, then left up Uz Pjacu which soon becomes Novi Put. Cross Hrvatskih Domobrana, where a sign points to *VIDOVA GORA* (**10min**). Continue up to cross the Bol–Supetar D115 road (**❶**; **15min**), where there's another *VIDOVA GORA* sign on the far side. Walk up the minor road called Donje Podbarje.

Continue up past 18th-century **Svete Josipa chapel** (**❷**) on the right, to a small **quarry** on the right and a *VIDOVA GORA* sign pointing along a track up the valley (**21min**). Shortly, at a minor junction, keep to the track; then, after about 10 minutes, bear right as it narrows to a **path** (**❸**; **35min**). Go through a simple gate, then up through a knot of tight zigzags. Almost immediately the valley closes in. Above is one of those rock formations that you can stare at for ages trying to decide what it resembles — a couchant lion perhaps? A little further on the path bends right and briefly leads southeastwards, affording a fine **view** (**❹**; **51min**) of Svete Ilija, goal of Walk 7. Beyond another bend and more zigzags, the path crosses a gully and continues up its left side (**1h10min**). In front of a large **pylon** bend right (**1h24min**). As the trees become more sparse, you pass a large shallow overhang (**1h50min**).

With the tops of the cliffs now close by, you're now on a track which bends left to parallel a **fence**

Looking south from the summit of Vidova Gora to Hvar

(**❺**; **2h**), as you cross the delightful plateau, dotted with pines. The towers on the summit appear and there's a superb view of Zlatni Rat below. Continue across the mosaic of limestone blocks, through a **gateway** (**❻**) to a car park. Take careful note of the location of the gateway — on the seaward side of the tower. Go through the gateway and up to the summit of **Vidova Gora** (**❼**; **2h16min**; Picnic 10), crowned with a large cross and communications towers. From a sign on the wall of the largest of these you learn that the mountain is named for St Vid, the remains of whose church lie in the vicinity.

After taking a break, retrace your steps to **Bol** (**4h30min**).

Walk 14 (Brač): BLACA MONASTERY FROM MURVICA

Distance/time: 20km/12mi; 6h20min

Grade: ● moderate, with approximately 460m/1509ft ascent. On roads, paths and tracks; waymarkers between Planica and Blaca Monastery

Equipment/map: see page 46; Trsat Auto Karte Dalmacija 2 (1:100,000)

Refreshments: available only in Murvica

Transport: 🚢 to Bol (see Transport, page 165, and notes on page 88 about parking). Then 🚗 to Murvica: from Bol, at the junction of the main D115 road and Hrvatskih Domobrana 0.5km northwest from the harbour, turn left towards MURVICA. After 2km turn right to MURVICA. There are two small parking areas 75m and 125m beyond Marija Bar (5km; 43° 15.975'N, 16° 35.595'E).

Nearest accommodation: Bol

Shorter walk: Blaca Monastery from the Vidova Gora road; see page 94.

The objective of this walk is the remote Glagolitic monastery at Blaca (see 'Glagolitic script', page 143), in an extraordinary location on the side of a rugged, isolated valley. It was funded in 1551 by priests from an inland area north of Split. The monastery is open daily except Monday from 8am to 3 (in low season) or 5pm in summer). From the hamlet of Murvica, at the foot of vertical dissected cliffs — a spectacular setting even by Croatian standards — the

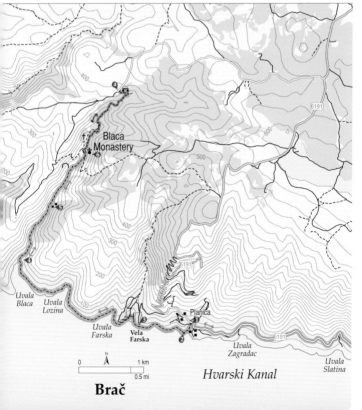

route also takes you past scattered settlements, vineyards vast and small, delightful coves and tiny shingle beaches, well away from any road. The walk starts at Murvica because there is nowhere to park safely and considerably further along the unsurfaced road.

Blaca Monastery

Set out from **Murvica** along the road which soon becomes unsurfaced (concreted on steep grades) and leads around deep **Uvala Dračeva**, with some ruined buildings high above at the foot of the cliffs. The unsurfaced road then leads on to **Uvala Slatina** (**40min**), with newly extensive young vineyards, and onwards above a small **headland** to the next indentation, shallow **Uvala Zagradac**. Just past the gated access to a house below left, fork left (**51min**). Continue past the **Terasa Ciccio** restaurant to a junction at **Planica** (❶; **1h10min**).

Here a faint waymarker and a sign on a rock point to BLACA. Go down the track ahead; fork left where a JENARO WINES sign is visible below. From that sign descend a steep track between vines to a path on top of a broad stone wall. Waymarkers appear intermittently from here. Then follow a stony path down, past a deserted building on the left. Turn right (❷) to continue through woodland. The path climbs from a shingle beach, briefly in the open, beside a stone wall. A little further on it's down to cross the shingle from where steps lead to a path which takes you into the hamlet of **Vela Farska** (❸; **1h40min**). Continue between deserted houses (there's a reassuring waymarker on the far side of house no 16) to a path that takes you up through woodland.

Go through a **gateway** and down through another **gate** to a tiny shingle beach, **Uvala Farska** (**1h45min**). Continue along the undulating path above the rocky shore, around **Uvala Lozina** (**2h5min**), a small inlet with two tiny and accessible shingle beaches separated by a low rock outcrop . The path leads on, soon turning into **Uvala Blaca** (❹; **2h35min**); go down a few steps, across rocks, to the shingle beach and, at the far end, head right up a signposted and waymarked path towards BLACA. This fine old, well-graded path rises through pines at first,

then more open ground. Beyond some **ruined buildings** (❺; **2h44min**) the cliffs close in and you pass through a narrow defile; on the far side look up to the left and you'll see a walled-in **cave** (**3h2min**). The gradient soon steepens and you catch the first glimpse of the monastery; the valley widens and you reach the threshold of **Blaca Monastery** (❻; **3h16min**) — its peace and tranquillity are almost palpable.

For the return, retrace your steps to **Murvica** (**6h20min**).

Shorter walk: Blaca Monastery from the Vidova Gora road;
3.6km/2.2mi; 50min. ● Easy, with 160m/525ft ascent; equipment as for the main walk. Access: from the road to Vidova Gora (see Car tour 3, Itinerary 1, page 19), turn right along the unsurfaced road signposted to BLACA (1km from the main D113 road. Follow it for a little over 2km, to a junction, similarly signposted, where you turn right on another unsurfaced road. After 4.5km you comes to a small parking area on the left by the signposted and waymarked **path to the monastery** (❼; 43° 18.082'N, 16° 32.132'E).

The wide path descends steadily, past deserted buildings on the left, into the valley. You pass a **cross** on the right and, beyond a stretch below vertical cliffs, continue up shallow steps to a path. Bear left here, to the entrance to **Blaca Monastery** (❻; **20min**).

For the return, retrace your steps to your car (**50min**).

HVAR: Introduction

Hvar has a reputation as a hedonistic, sun-soaked resort, but there is of course much more to the island, for walkers in particular. The most prominent feature of the landscape is an elongated east-west limestone ridge, its southern slopes tumbling into the sea, the northern flanks giving way more gradually to a broad coastal plain. The ridge is topped by Svete Nikola, at 628m the highest point on the island. It was the fertile plain that beckoned Greek settlers who arrived in 384BC and set up shop at Pharos, now Stari Grad. They were followed by the Romans; Hvar was later crucial to the Venetian empire as a naval base. Cultivation of vineyards (with white wine grapes on the plain, red on the southern slopes), olive groves and orchards thrived from the beginning, and still do, if on a smaller scale. These features are the focus of the three walks in this section, from a base at Stari Grad, less frenetic than Hvar town, but still with all the facilities visitors might need. The walks cover exploration of Stari Grad plain (a UNESCO world heritage site), the not unduly strenuous ascent of Svete Nikola and a tour of two venerable villages linked to a scenic coastal path. Signposting and some waymarking make these walks easy enough to follow. The island is well served by its local bus services and is on the route of frequent catamaran and car ferry services to the mainland and other islands in the southern Adriatic.

Photo: Stari Grad harbour

Walk 15 (Hvar): STARI GRAD PLAIN

Distance/time: 8.6km/5.3mi; 2h25min
Grade: ● easy, with approximately 65m/215ft of ascent. On quiet roads and tracks and a short path; some signposts
Equipment/map: see page 46; walking shoes suitable; Stari Grad leaflet 'Walking through History' (1:40,000)
Refreshments: available in Stari Grad

Transport: 🚢 ferry or catamaran to Stari Grad/Hvar town, 🚐 or 🚌 to Stari Grad (see Transport, page 165). There is a large pay car park next to the Stari Grad bus station (43° 11.112'N, 16° 36.032'E).
Nearest accommodation: Stari Grad, Hvar town
Note: This walk is particularly bike-friendly (apart from the section from waypoint ⑥); bikes can be hired in Stari Grad.

Stari Grad Plain is a UNESCO World Heritage Site, between Stari Grad and Vrboska, set aside in 2008 to protect the settlement pattern laid out and built by Greek colonisers from about 384 BC, and named Pharos. It comprises rectangular plots defined by stone walls, dissected horizontally and lengthwise by straight roads, known as *chora,* and including a rainwater conservation system. Through the Roman era, Middle Ages and beyond the area was intensely cultivated, mainly with vineyard, olive groves and lavender fields, all three still carried on.

The roads, now vehicle tracks, make for easy walking (or cycling) and, with the help of on-site interpretation, offer the unusual experience (in Croatia at least) of experiencing a landscape that, essentially, has scarcely changed in more than two millennia.

From the **tourist office** at the head of **Stari Grad harbour** (**O**), head off eastwards, then take the first street left and shortly diverge to the park and follow a path parallel to the road. At the far end cross the road and continue in the same direction along Put Gospojice, a litte offset to the right. At a **sub-station** (**①**), keep ahead at the junction. Within 150m the road becomes a wide track. This is Put Demetrija Farskog, named after a notable Greek official. You pass a small 16th-century chapel, **Gospojica** (**②; 35min**), standing

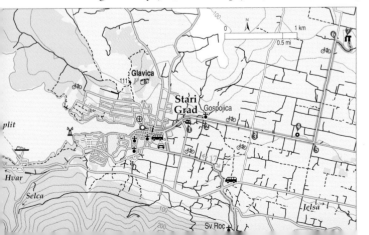

Wine barrels on the plain and the 16th-century Gospojica chapel

discreetly in a corner on the left, and then the junction with **Komon's Path** dating from the 3rd century BC, also on the left (**❸**; **45min**). Many of the surrounding fields are now cultivated with vines and olives. A few minutes further on there's a shady bench and an information board.

Two tall poplars mark the location of a large, well-preserved **trim** (**❹**) on the left. These stone structures, built without any form of cement and with domed ceilings and low entrances facing west, are common throughout southern Europe. These probably date back to Greek and Roman times, though some were built as late as the 19th century. They are used for shelter and storing tools (see also Walk 17, page 101).

Further along the track turn left along 4th-century **Matijeu Put** (**❺**). This junction is at the crux of the Greek scheme of measurement for the division of the plain into fields. This track rises slightly to a junction (**❻**; **1h18min**) where a path leads between stone walls towards an archaeological site.

At another junction (**1h26min**) turn left on a path to **Maslinovik** (note the small trim on the right here). The remains of the base of a 4th-century BC Greek watchtower are clearly discernible, surrounded by much more recent small stone buildings. The views of the wide valley, Dol village and the Svete Nikola ridge (Walk 17) are superb.

Now retrace your steps to **Stari Grad** (**2h25min**).

97

Walk 16 (Hvar): FROM VELO GRABLJE TO HVAR TOWN

Distance/time: 11.2km/7mi; 4h
Grade: ● easy-moderate, with 350m/1148ft descent and approximately 50m/164ft ascent; on quiet roads, unsurfaced roads, tracks, paths and shingle (with some rock hopping). Waymarked/signposted to Uvala Poklonji Dol
Equipment/map: see page 46; Kartograf map of Hvar (1:75,000)
Refreshments: available at Milna, Robinson, Uvala Pokonji Dol (seasonal), and Hvar town
Transport: 🚢 to Hvar, then 🚌 from Hvar town to the turn-off for Velo Grablje (see Transport, page 165).
Nearest accommodation: Hvar town

Shorter walks
1 Velo Grablje to Milna; 4.3km/2.7mi; 1h27min. ● Easy, with 350m/1148ft descent; equipment and transport as for the main walk; return to Hvar town by 🚌 (15min; see Transport, page 165). Follow the main walk to **Milna** (❺), then return to the main D116 for the bus (❹).
2 Milna to Hvar town; 7km/4.3mi; 2h33min. ● Easy, with approximately 50m/164ft ascent; equipment as for the main walk. Transport: see page 165 for the bus to Milna; the stop is on the main D116 (❹). Follow the main walk to **Milna** (❺) and from there back to **Hvar** town (❾).

This is a walk marked by extraordinary contrasts, from Hvar's high, breezy ridge, through old villages and olive groves, to rocky shores and shingle beaches. The two villages, Velo and Malo Grablje, are living examples of changes that have been happening on Hvar for decades, especially away from the tourist-favoured coast. Prolonged decline may, until recently, have been terminal, but now there are definite signs of renewal. The two parts of the walk, inland and coast, can be explored separately over two days, either by using the bus — or as out-and-back walks by car.

Ideally, start the walk from the **Vidikovac Levanda** restaurant (❶; see Car tour 4, page 20) which is a very few hundred metres uphill from the bus stop (the driver might be willing to drop you here, on request). The alternative — of walking down the road to Velo Grablje — is much less attractive. From the restaurant

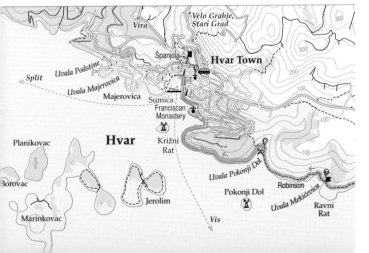

set out along a waymarked track signposted to VELO GRABLJE and other destinations. At a junction turn right, soon with a good view of the **Pakleni Islands** off Hvar town. Pass an old **reservoir** on the right (**10min**), similar to those on Walk 20, Paklenica National Park, page 112, then a large cross. Continue down; bearing left between two stone buildings and down a concrete road to a T-junction, where you turn left.

Then you come to the large plain **church** in **Velo Grablje**, opposite which is the well-preserved village **co-operative**, founded in 1892 and the first of its kind in Croatia, where you can inspect the original olive mill.

Follow the waymarkers downhill; press on to the right (**24min**) on a wide grassed path that bends left into a narrow valley. Go straight on at a junction on the right (**29min**). Cross the stream bed, go up to a road (**❷**; **38min**) and turn left. With olive groves on either side — some of the trees appear to be extremely old, judging by the size of the trunks — you come to a junction below the hamlet of **Malo Grablje** (**52min**). Here, and a little further on at a road junction, signs describe features nearby and in the village

which dates from about the 16th century. It's certainly worth the diversion to potter about among the buildings, many still remarkably intact, if overgrown.

Continue down the road between olive groves. When you come to a junction, keep left on a track. *(But for Shorter walk 1 bear right up to the main D116, where the bus stop is nearby to the right at* **❹** *)* The main walk keeps ahead down the track and through a tunnel under the D116 (**50min**), and on to the shore in the large coastal village of **Milna** (**❺**; **1h27min**).

Follow signs to HVAR and other places, and waymarkers along a minor road to the right through a campsite, to an attractive beach. Cross the shingle and, near the far end, bear right up a path with waymarkers. Then bear right and uphill on a wide rocky path; through olive groves it becomes an earthen track, still climbing. Turn left (**1h47min**) towards MEKICEVICA. Red waymarkers then indicate a sharp right bend (**1h55min**) to a junction, where you turn left. The narrow path leads through dense bushes and out into coastal heathland; it soon descends slightly, close to the rocky shore, to tiny **Uvala Katolić** (**❻**). Walk across the boulders, smooth

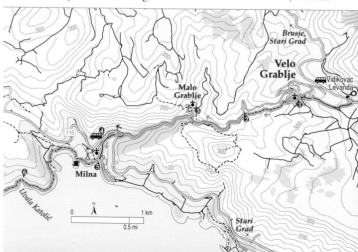

Malo Grablje (above) and the Hvar uplands (left)

wide path to **Uvala Mekićevica** (**7**; **2h22min**). Bear right for 'Robinson', a rustic café, or left for the beach .

From the café, go up steps to the left, through a **gate**, to a path. Soon you're back down on a beach, this one with rounded, bleached shingle. Go up, across rocks, to a path which runs through trees at first, then in the open. Bear left downhill to traverse a low cliff below a small olive grove, then the shore's edge. Follow **blue waymarkers** through trees, across a short rocky stretch, and on to **Uvala Pokonji Dol** (**8**; **2h52min**), from where a minor road takes you back to Hvar town. It's shaded by pines at first, then passes houses, a bay full of small boats, the Franciscan monastery and a small cove, before leading on to Riva and Trg Svete Stepana in **Hvar town** (**9**; **4h**).

and crumbly, then bear right along a path into the bush. Beyond a couple of bends, it turns inland to bypass the extremity of the head-land, **Ravni Rat**. Then descend a

100

Walk 17 (Hvar): SVETE NIKOLA SUMMIT FROM STARI GRAD

Distance/time: 18km/11.2mi; 5h25min (from Stari Grad); 14km/8.7mi; 4h05min (from Dol)
Grade: ● moderate, with 628m/2060ft ascent (528m/1732ft from Dol). On quiet minor roads, paths and tracks; intermittent sign-posting and waymarking
Equipment: see page 46; walking poles
Refreshments: available in Stari Grad and Dol (bar only)
Transport: 🚢 ferry or catamaran to Stari Grad/Hvar town, 🚐 or 🚌 to Stari Grad (see Transport, page 165). There is a large pay car park next to the Stari Grad bus station (43° 11.112'N, 16° 36.032'E). Alternatively, 🚌 to Dol, where there is *limited* parking (except on Sundays and Holy days) beside the

prominent Svete Mihovil church (43° 10.130'N, 16° 37.107'E). Or park at the bar at Dol (❸) — being sure to give them your custom! (*Note that* buses on the Stari Grad–Vrboska–Jelsa route *may* diverge via Dol on request.
Nearest accommodation: Stari Grad, Hvar town
Shorter walk: Svete Nikola view; 10km/6.2mi; 3h14min (from Stari Grad); 5km/3mi; 2h12min (from Dol). ● Easy, with approximately 320m/1050ft ascent from Stari Grad) or 220m/722ft from Dol; equipment and transport as for the main walk. Follow the main walk to the 2h7min-mark at ❺, for good views of Svete Nikola on the skyline, then retrace steps to the start.

Hvar's landscape is dominated by the long, generally east-west ridge which rises precipitously from the sea and slopes steeply northwards. The highest point, Svete Nikola (628m), south of Stari Grad, commands an extraordinarily wide-ranging view — from the island of Mljet to the Biokovo mountains and the outskirts of Split. The route to the summit traverses olive groves, shady woodlands and, in the upper reaches, bare hillsides. The short walk, to a scenic viewpoint above the village of Dol, offers a sample of some of the scenery on the longer walk.

Start out from the **bus stop** (or adjacent car park) in **Stari Grad** (**O**): walk south along the minor road (Put Kriza) to a T-junction and turn left. Shortly, cross an intersection and continue east then southeast along what is Selino's Path, part of the ancient network on Stari Grad Plain dating from at least the 3rd century BC (see Walk 15, page 96). Then you come to a small medieval **church** (**❶**) dedicated to St Helena. Cross the Hvar–Jelsa D116 road and, 300m further on, bear right (**❷**) to walk into **Dol**. Go straight ahead at the

next two junctions, and you will come to the **bus stop** (**❸**) and a bar on the right. From the bar go uphill and around a bend. Turn right up a concrete road called Glavica which leads to **Svete Mihovil church** (**❹**; **55min**).

Continue to the right, as indicated by a waymarker. Soon the road gives way to a track, then path, continuing the climb. At the **1h32min** mark you'll find a well-preserved stone-built **trim** (see Walk 15, page 97). Next you come to a left bend at a junction (**1h50min**). A brief change of

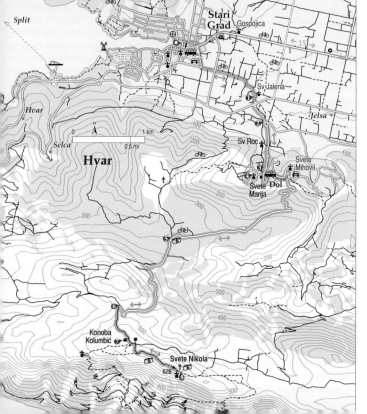

View north from the cross on Svete Nikola (above left); wild sage (above) and tree heather (left), seen on many walks

retrace your steps.) Then, as the track drops into a valley of open grassland dotted with pines, the towns of Vrboska and Jelsa hove into view.

At a track junction (**❻**; **2h29min**) turn left for SVETE NIKOLA and continue up to a broad saddle (**2h40min**) where you'll find the family-run **Konoba Kolumbić** (**❼**). In front of a nearby house, turn right. Shortly, a steep concrete path leads to the final climb on a rocky path, past a small stone building, beyond which is the highly visible cross and **Svete Nikola chapel** on the summit (**❽**; **3h**). During spring the summit ridge is adorned by many species of colourful wildflowers.

From here retrace your steps to **Stari Grad** (**5h25min**).

scene is provided by a meadow packed with thick stone walls and huge clearance cairns and which offers a good view of Brac and the small town of Bol. Very soon the surroundings open up and Svete Nikola, topped by a cross, comes into view (**❺**; **2h7min**). *(The Shorter walk returns from here: just*

Walk 18 (Plitvice Lakes National Park): CIRCUIT OF THE LAKES AND FALLS

Distance/time: 8.5km/5.3mi; 4h; add 2.7km/1.7mi; 30min if you walk from P3 back to P1 (see text)
Grade: ● easy, with approximately 50m/164m ascent, on paths and boardwalks, liberally signposted (identified by an alphabetical colour-coded scheme, illustrated on large signs at key junctions).
Equipment/map: see page 46; walking shoes suitable; water-proofs for Veliki Slap; Plitvice Lakes National Park map (1:50,000). *Notes:* On maps and in the text, 'P1-3' are ferry landings; 'ST1-3' are stops for the internal national park buses. On our map waypoints and symbols are minimal to avoid confusion; there are viewpoints all along.
Entrance ticket: *It's vital that you purchase an entry ticket online no less than two days before your visit.* Otherwise you may miss out or have to queue for a long time. Entrance is managed to ensure both the protection of the park's fragile environment and an enjoyable experience for visitors. For full details go to the park's website (www.np-plitvicka-jezera.hr).
Refreshments: available at Entrance 2, P3 and ST3
Transport: 🚌 (see Transport, page 165) or 🚗 to the park (Car tour 6). Park at entrance 2 (the more southerly), on the eastern side of the main road (44° 53.024'N, 15° 37.411'E). Cross this via a foot-bridge and follow signs to P1. Electric boats shuttle between P1 and P2 and between P2 and P3. Check times of last departures.
Nearest accommodation: Plitvice Jezera (hotels only) opposite entrance 2; Mukinje (2km south); Korana (△; 6km north).
Short walk: Veliki Slap; 3km/ 1.8mi; 50min. ● Easy; equipment as main walk. Follow the main walk to ❶, return to P3, take a boat to P2, then another to P1.

Plitvice Lakes National Park is undoubtedly one of the two or three finest natural features in Croatia (see panel opposite). It is, inevitably, extremely popular, and even in spring you'll run into slow-moving clusters of visitors. However, it's easy to escape the crowds and enjoy some of the fascinating waterfalls and cascades and the incomparably beautiful lakes in comparative peace. The route outlined here is not the only one possible, but it should enable you to navigate the path identification scheme and to visit all the lakes and waterfalls.

To start the walk, catch a boat from P1 to P2 then another (from 8.30am) to **P3** (❍) at the northern end of **Jezero Kozjak**. Walk up the road from a souvenir shop for 50m to a path on the right (F, H; brown) signposted to *VELIKI SLAP*. Go up to a road then turn right; descend to a boardwalk across the outlet from Jezero Kozjak. Turn left with routes F, H. A wide path drops down to the shore of **Jezero Milanovac** with cliffs right beside you. Go down beside **Slap Milke Trnine** and continue beside **Jezero Gavanovack**, then across to the western shore of **Kaluderovac Jezero**. At a junction where 'St1' is signed to the right, go straight on (F, H) beside the cliff to a large **viewing area** (❶; **30min**) at the base of magnificent **Veliki Slap**.

Mali Prštavac

TRAVERTINE

Plitvice Lakes National Park (www.np-plitvicka-jezera.hr) is probably Croatia's most outstanding natural attraction and absolutely unmissable. Nearly 80% is forested, but the chain of 16 lakes, linked by cascades and waterfalls, is truly exceptional. Indeed the park was declared a Unesco World Heritage Site in 1979. The lakes and cascades are hypnotically beautiful — constantly changing colour through every imaginable shade of blue and green. Its special status, however, derives from the formation of *travertine* or *tufa* — a biodynamic process ongoing for millennia. Water erodes and dissolves the rocks; the calcium carbonate solution stimulates mosses, algae and freshwater plants to produce a sediment. This accumulates as travertine, a white encrustation on logs and branches, and as ever-changing barriers between the lakes.

Visitors began arriving at the lakes at the end of the 19th century; the park was set aside in 1949. Ominously, the Homeland War erupted here in 1991, and the park was occupied by Serbian forces until 1995. The infrastructure was destroyed but everything else left unharmed. The park is extremely well organised to cope with large numbers of visitors and to ensure the protection of its natural features.

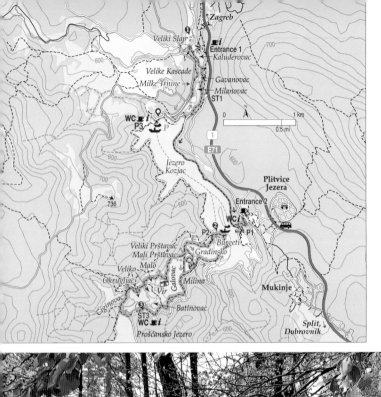

To vary the return, I recommend the route discreetly signed A, B, C (green) and K (green/brown). Climb steep steps and traverse a **tunnel**, to reach the ridge. A path to the right leads to a superb **lookout** over the falls. Return to the main path, which parallels the cliff edge above the features of the outward route, through beech forest, with more viewpoints along the way. When you come to a road bear left; in a few hundred metres, as you pass a park entrance gate, continue straight on. Turn right at a junction and go down to join your outward route near **P3** (**1h**).

Rather than wait for boats, you can walk back to **P1** (allow about **30min** extra). Retrace steps to the Jezero Kozjak outlet then turn

right along a shoreside road for about 100m. Go right down a path signed to P1 – a very pleasant, peaceful alternative.

From **P1** take a boat to **P2** (**❷**). Follow route C up steps to the right, then via a boardwalk across rushing torrents to the far end of **Lake Burgeti**. A shoreside path leads on beside the larger **Lake Gradinsko**; at its far end continue straight on (H, K) by the shore. Pass through drifts of fine spray from **Veliki Prštavac** (**1h30min**) cascading over a wavy cliff. Just past **Galovački Buk**, turn right at a junction (E, C) towards ST3. Gain a little height to another junction where you continue straight on beside **Jezero Galovac** (H, K) seemingly vast by comparison (**2h10min**). At the far end go up beside a tributary stream and around to a junction then follow E, C up to **ST3** (**❸**; **2h35min**).

Continue with route H, soon along a boardwalk, briefly beside **Proscanko Jezero**. Cross a meadow, walk past **Ciginovac** below, then along a boardwalk across its outlet stream spilling into **Okrugljak**.

At a junction (**3h**) where HIKING TRAILS diverge to the left, go straight on (H, K, P2). Shortly, at a junction turn right (H, K) and descend beside **Malo Jezero** to enjoy superb views across **Jezero Galovac**. At the next intersection at the end of that lake, go straight on along routes H, K (**3h15min**). Then you pass tiny **Milino Jezero**, a dry depression, and **Gradinsko Jezero**. Finally, there's **Jezero Burgeti** and the descent back to **P2** (**4h**).

Jerzero **Okrugljak**

Set aside in 1949, the park is dominated by two spectacular canyons: Velika Paklenica and Mala Paklenica, 14km and 12km long respectively and about 400m deep. With an altitude range from 50m along its southern boundary to the summit of Vaganski (1757m) on the crest of the Velebit mountain range, the park protects a wealth of flora and fauna in 20 different habitats. Of these, rocks and cliffs are widespread, hosting ferns, bellflower and buckthorn. Two-thirds of the park's area is forested, where the main species are European beech, holm oak, white hornbeam and white and black pine. The sap of the last-named gave the park its name. The beech forests were inscribed on the World Heritage List in 2017, being part of the ancient and primeval beech forests of the Carpathian mountains. Paklenica is also within the Velebit Biosphere Reserve declared in 1978, and is a member of Natura 2000, a Europe-wide network of preserved areas, the largest such in the world. The park is home to several endangered bird species including Eurasian vulture and peregrine falcon (see 'Beli' on page 33) and numerous mammals.

Evidence of prehistoric occupation has been found within the park, while Velika Paklenica is an ancient trade route, and until the 1950s there were several working mills in the area (see Short 'picnic' walk 22, page 42 and Walk 20, page 112).

The Velika Paklenica cliffs are among Europe's top rock climbing venues; the annual Big Wall speed climbing competition on 1st May draws climbers from around the world.

The park is very popular but with 150km of marked routes, peace and quiet are not elusive. The walks described offer an introduction to its magnificent landscape, its natural and historical features and all should be within the reach of reasonably fit walkers.

For more information, consult www.paklenica.hr.

Photo: Entrance to Paklenica National Park

Walk 19 (Paklenica National Park): VELIKA PAKLENICA AND PLANINARSKI DOM PAKLENICA

Distance/time: 14.5km/8.7mi; 4h30min from park entrance station; 10.5km/6.3mi (3h30min) from upper car park; add 7.2km/4.3mi (2h) if you walk from Starigrad-Paklenica.

Grade: ● easy-moderate with 410m/1345ft ascent; on quiet road, trails and paths, signposted and waymarked

Equipment/map: see page 46; walking poles. Drinking water may be available along the way (see '*Voda*' and ♪ symbol on the map); Paklenica National Park Mountain Map (1:25,000)

Refreshments: available near the upper car park, at Lugarnica forest cottage, Planinarski Dom Paklenica, and Ramica Dvori (near the Dom), plus nearby village of Marasovići and in Starigrad-Paklenica

Transport: 🚌 (Car tour 6)): the road to the park entrance is signposted on the A8 highway on the eastern edge of Starigrad-Paklenica. Drive north for just over 1km to the entrance station, where you buy an entry ticket (one-day or multi-

day passes are available). There is a car park here and several more up to another 2km further north (which fill up quickly at weekends). Or **on foot** from Starigrad-Paklenica via Velebitska Ulica (an Educational Trail); there are three approaches, from west to east: 1) simply follow Velebitska Ulica from the eastern side of Hotel Viko; 2) join it via Razanačka Ulica near the tourist office; 3) take Ulica Ante Starčevica. For options 2 and 3 turn right along Velebitska Ulica when you meet it and continue through the village of Marasovići. Turn left for 300m to the park entrance.

Nearest accommodation: Starigrad-Paklenica; mountain refuge Planinarski Dom Paklenica

Shorter walk: Lugaranica forest cottage; 11.4km/7.2mi. ● Easy, with 380m/1246ft ascent on signposted and waymarked trails. Equipment and transport as for the main walk. Follow the main walk to the **cottage** (❻; **1h45min**), then retrace steps to the start.

The awesome walls and cliffs of Velika Paklenica (see panel opposite) are memorably impressive from the floor of the canyon where you feel positively dwarfed by their enormity. Indeed, it seems miraculous that you can walk through with comparative ease. The wide trail is endowed with several information boards describing the outstanding ecological and cultural importance of the canyon and the park generally. Bear in mind that Walk 21 (page 115) offers the opportunity to fully appreciate the scale of the canyon and the surrounding peaks and ridges.

Start the walk at the **park entrance** (**O**) or the **upper car park** (❹) and follow the road, past cliffs much sought-after by rock climbers, in **Velika Paklenica** canyon. From the upper car park,

the road gives way to a wide stone-paved trail then a track. About 400m beyond the car park, you pass a **Presentation Centre** (❶) featuring 'The Underground Secrets of Paklenica' — restored bunkers originally built for Marshall Tito between 1950-1953. It has coffee and souvenir shops and is open daily May-September.

The trail is quieter beyond the climbing zone; the canyon widens to a wooded amphitheatre and you pass a possible **water source** (❷). The track levels out and you pass a grassy clearing on the right, a potential rest place where you may even notice that the climbers' shouts have been replaced by bird calls. Ignore the turn-off to Manita Peć (❸; **1h10min**; Walk 21).

Soon the sweeping barrier of peaks and cliffs above the head of the valley comes into view; through beech and oak woodland, you come to another potential

water source (❹; **1h30min**). Continue, past the turnoff to 'Veliko Rujino' (❺) and various information boards, to **Lugarnica Foresters Cottage** (❻; **1h45min**) just to the left of the main track. More information boards about the park provide distractions en route to **Planinarski Dom Paklenica** (❼; **2h15min**).

There are several outdoor picnic tables here, otherwise the chalet-style building could provide welcome shelter. An alternative **refreshment stop** (❽; **Ramica Dvori**) is attractively signposted just up to the right.

To return, retrace your steps, as ever quite a different experience from the outward walk (**4h30min**).

Photo: in Velika Paklenica canyon

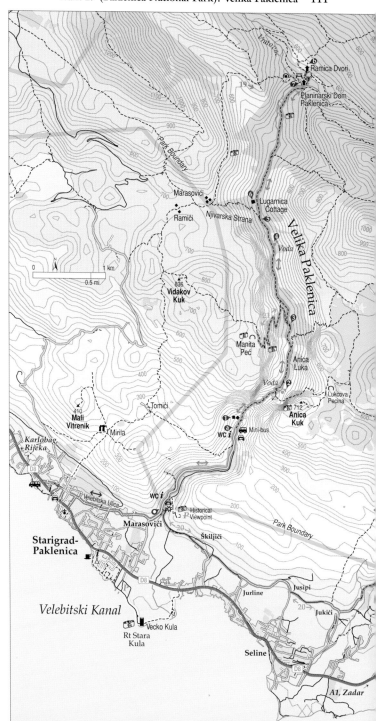

Walk 20 (Paklenica National Park): A SHORT WALK THROUGH HISTORY AND MALA PAKLENICA

Distance/time: 9km/5.4mi; 3h from the Velika Paklenica park entrance station
Grade: ● easy with about 30m ascent on paths, tracks, quiet roads; signposted and waymarked
Equipment/map: see page 46; walking shoes or sandals suitable; Paklenica National Park Mountain Map (1:25,000)
Refreshments: available in Marasoviči and near the upper car park
Transport: see Walk 19, page 109, and park at the entrance to Velika Paklenica. There is also a car park at the entrance to Mala Paklenica, in case you want to do the walk in reverse: access to Mala Paklenica is

about 3km southeast of the Velika Paklenica access road off the D8. The road leads north for 1.3km to the Mala Paklenica car park (44° 16.977'N, 15° 29.585'E). Most of this walk is just *outside* the national park, but it starts and finishes at the Velika Paklenica park entrance and re-enters the park at the Mala Paklenica park entrance.
Nearest accommodation: Starigrad-Paklenica, Seline
Short walk: Educational Trail; 1.2km/0.7mi; 30min. ● Easy, with minimal ascent; equipment and transport as for the main walk. Follow the main walk to ❷ and return the same way.

Educational Trails have become popular in Croatia and some are featured in this book (Short 'picnic' walk 22, page 42; part of Walk 4, page 62 and most of Walk 27, page 132). Here, local history is divided into five sections: three covering prehistory, one for Roman rule and the last, the Middle Ages to 19th century. Excellently designed, with an English version, using maps and illustrations and set in their general context, they offer a very effective introduction to the ebb and flow of regimes and ways of life, more memorable than printed or digital presentations in isolation. The landscape and human activities have changed with fluctuating sea levels from prehistoric hunter-gatherers to herders and later traders. Evidence of many of these themes can be found within the park. The walk has three distinct parts: the history trail, a string of traditional villages where there are signs of contemporary rejuvenation, and the dramatic entrance to Mala Paklenica gorge.

At the park entrance a wooden sign, *POUCNA STAZA*, points the way to the right (**O**). (If you walked here along Velebitska Ulica from Starigrad-Paklenica this sign should be familiar.) Cross a bridge and follow the track, bending right. On the left is the **Lower Marasovic mill** (**❶**) with a large millstone outside. Cross another bridge and go up to a junction;

Mala Paklenica entrance station, with the canyon in the background

bear left with a sign for the TRAIL and close by a **large board** introducing it. Then go right along a clearly defined track between stone walls. As the view ahead opens up, you come to the **second board** covering the years 6000-2000BC. Just ahead at a fork bear right along a gravel path with fine views of the Velebit Channel. Then in quick succession are the **third** (Bronze and Iron Ages) and **fourth** (Roman Empire) **boards**.

A few minutes further on, the path merges with a trail on the left, and then you reach the **fifth and last board** (❷; Venetians to Austro-Hungarian Empire). This one is of particular interest for the illustrated ruin of Vecka Kula, in plain view (**15min**; see Short 'picnic' walk 21, page 41). *(The shorter walk returns from here.)*

About 200m ahead, continue on a road through the settlement of **Škiljići-Dadići** (❸), now

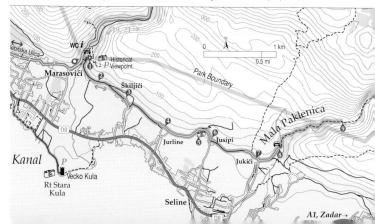

mostly deserted but still illustrative of traditional building styles.

At a T-junction turn left with a TRAIL sign; gain some height as the road bends right and a gravel trail leads on. Further on, a large concrete structure on the right is a cistern for gathering rainwater for the local communities, used during 19th and early 20th centuries.

Next you pass **Jurline** (**④**), where some old stone buildings have been restored. If you look back here you'll catch a good view of Vecka Kula in the distance while ahead and to the right is the bridge across the Velebit Channel to the Zadar peninsula.

The track gains some height; at a junction keep right and perhaps pause at an informal **viewpoint** (**⑤**) over Seline. Go on downhill; look out for a small cistern on the left, and soon reach a road. In front of the first house on the left in **Jusipi** (**⑥**; **1h**), turn left along a track with a TRAIL sign. Pass a cluster of substantial old stone buildings on the left flanked by a patchwork of small, stone-walled fields. Soon you'll see a large new (or restored) stone house on the left with fields planted with figs, olives, lavender and fruit trees. Then you come to **Jukići** (**⑦**), complete with street lights. At a junction with a sign to MALA PAKLENICA, turn left.

Shortly the almost forbidding entrance to the canyon looms ahead and you reach the **park entrance station** (**⑧**; **1h10min**)

with the ticket office, small Educational Centre featuring birds of prey in protected areas, and toilets.

To gain an idea of just how narrow the canyon is (as little as 10m in some places), follow a narrow rocky path parallel to the stream, which may be dry. Soon you cross a dry channel and continue on the path through white pine and juniper. Apart from near the car park, lunch spots are few, but about 50m beyond a sign warning about rock falls, an open area offers possibilities; beyond here the path becomes rough and rocky (**⑨**; **1h30min**).

To return, simply retrace your steps — the views always look different on the way back (**3h**).

Walk 21 (Paklenica National Park): MANITA PEČ

Distance: 8.8km/5.4mi; 3h40min; add 7.2km/4.3mi; 1h 30min if you walk from Starigrad-Paklenica
Grade: ● easy-moderate with 520m/1706ft ascent on quiet roads, trails and paths; signposted and waymarked

Equipment/map: see page 46; walking poles; Paklenica National Park Mountain Map (1:25,000)
Refreshments: available near the upper car park, in Marasovići and Starigrad-Paklenica
Transport: as Walk 19, page 109

Manita Peć is the only one of the 70 caves in Paklenica National Park that is open to visitors - accompanied by a guide. The cave, comprising two vast chambers, is 175m long and 35m deep; the path is easy to follow and adequately lit. It's open daily July-September, otherwise Monday, Wednesday and Saturday April-June and October, 10.00-14.00; buy your ticket at the on-site office.

As well as several species of bats, 20 species of specially adapted, colourless and sightless animals live in the cave.

Walkways in Manita Peć

The exceptionally beautiful formations include stalagmites, stalagtites and columns.

The well-designed path from the canyon up to the cave and nearby lookout introduces you to wildlife habitats different from those below. The more open woodlands comprise hornbeam and holm oak, and the cliffs and crags above with ferns, bellflower and sandwort. Birds you're likely to see include chaffinch and nightingale; among the mammals are badger and pine marten. From the lookout, just 100m short of the cave, the spectacular panorama embraces the depths of the canyon and the major peaks in the park, crowned by Vaganski at 1757m.

Start the walk at the **park entrance** (**O**) or the **upper car park** (**a**) and follow the road, past cliffs much sought-after by rock climbers, in **Velika Paklenica** canyon. From the upper car park, the road gives way to a wide stone-paved trail then a track. About 400m beyond the car park, you pass a **Presentation Centre** (**❶**) featuring restored bunkers originally built for Marshall Tito between 1950-1953. It has coffee and souvenir shops and is open daily May-September.

The tar soon ends and the trail becomes quieter beyond the cliffs; the canyon widens to a wooded amphitheatre and you pass a possible **water source** (**❷**).

The turnoff to Manita Peć is clearly signposted (**❸**; **1h10min**). Long zigzags make the ascent easy enough; nearing the base of the cliffs, the switchbacks shorten; increasingly wide views reward your effort along the way and several information boards provide good reasons to pause. Beyond a cleft you reach a perfectly-sited **viewpoint** (**❹**; **1h55min**), almost within sight of the entrance to **Manita Peć** (**❺**).

From here retrace your steps to the **park entrance** (**3h40min**) or your starting point.

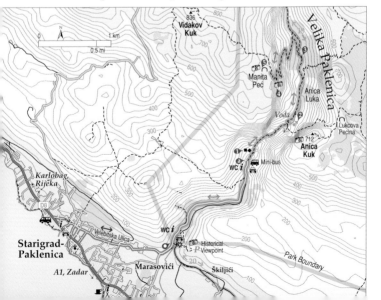

KVARNER GULF: *Introduction*

The mountainous Učka massif, part of the Dinaric Alps, rises steeply from the head of the Kvarner Gulf southwest of Rijeka and dominates the view northwards from the islands of Cres and Krk. It culminates in the very accessible peak of Vojak (1396m) and provides a dramatic, forested backdrop to the historic coastal towns and villages below. The massif lies within Učka Nature Park, a large reserve set aside in 1999 to protect its distinctive geology, plentiful wildlife, including many endemic and endangered species, and to support the small communities and their cultural heritage, particularly music and song, within its boundaries. Limestone is the main, almost only rock type; there are about 200 caves and sinkholes, and numerous springs which make an invaluable contribution to the local water supply. The lower slopes support forests of holm oak, hornbeam and the culturally important sweet chestnut; higher up, beech is the dominant species, taking on a stunted form along the ridge crest. Wildlife is abundant, if elusive; red squirrels favour the chestnut for its nesting holes, while you may spot a golden eagle or peregrine falcon high above.

The park is endowed with an extensive network of well-marked paths and trails, including an Educational Trail on the summit ridge. The walks described here offer an introduction to the park's features, together with the historic and justly famous coastal path between Volosko and Lovran, from which the massif is often in view.

For more information consult the park's excellent website, www.pp-ucka.hr.

Photo: Maiden with seagull (Walk 22)

Walk 22 (Kvarner Gulf): FROM VOLOSKO TO LOVRAN VIA OPATIJA

Distance/time: 10km/6mi; 2h40min
Grade: ● easy; no appreciable ascent; on paths and minor roads
Equipment/map: see page 46; swimming things, trekking sandals/walking shoes suitable; Rima Leisure map of the Opatija Riviera (1:35,000)
Refreshments: abundantly available from start to finish
Transport: 🚌 32 from Lovran to Volosko (see Transport, page 165); alight at the second stop above Volosko

Nearest accommodation: Opatija, Lovran
Shorter walks
1 Volosko to Opatija; 2.7km/1.6mi; 1h. ● Easy. The Opatija bus station is beside the very prominent Grand Hotel Palace and about 100m inland. End the coastal walk at ❸.
2 Opatija to Lovran; 7.3km/4.4mi; 1h40min. ● Easy; transport as for main walk; alight at Opatija and follow the main walk to the end. Start at ❸.

D uring the late 19th and early 20th centuries, the Opatija Riviera was the playground of the Austro-Hungarian nobility, while the villages and small towns thrived to serve their needs and as busy commercial centres. Villas and landscaped gardens endure as monuments to the imperial past, and most are beautifully preserved. The shoreside promenade, named after Emperor Franz Josef I, opened in 1899 from Volosko to Opatija and was extended to Lovran in 1911. Numerous plaques and information boards beside the path commemorate noted visitors and residents: musicians, scientists and others, and bring to life the history of the villages as ports, the long-forgotten Rijeka–Opatija railway and much else. The path is best walked from north to south for the views of the Učka mountain range and the islands of Cres and Krk. Toilets (for a small fee) are plentiful, as are safe places for swimming.

Near Ičići

Start at the **bus stop** on the main road above **Volosko** (**O**): walk downhill along Ulica Dr Ivana Poščića to an intersection; cross the road on the left and descend the steps of Ulica Skradinje to the shore in the village centre. Beyond a handful of restaurants and the small harbour, turn a corner to join Obalno Šetalište Franza Josefa I (**15min**).

Of the several beaches en route, **Plaža Tomasevac** (**❶**; **45min**), just north of Opatija, has earned a Blue Flag. Soon you come to **Opatija harbour**. As the path bends left below an ochre-coloured villa, go up steps on the right, cross the road and enter **Park Angiolina** (**❷**). This beautiful, shady retreat is blessed with a great variety of trees, a few secluded seats and the wonderful neo-classical, mid-19th century Villa Angiolina where you may find an art exhibition. Keep to paths bearing left, and you should emerge almost in front of the dazzling Hotel Kvarner, probably the oldest hotel on the Adriatic coast, opened in 1884. On the next small headland is **Park Svetog Jakova** (**❸**; **1h**), another, although less secluded oasis. (*Shorter walk 1 finishes and Shorter walk 2 starts here.*)

Just offshore at the next small point is Opatija's trademark, the statue of **Das Mädchen mit der Möwe** (**❹**; The Maiden with the Seagull, shown on page 117). The path leads on through quieter, often shady surroundings; around a bend, the Učka mountains come into view.

A little further on, go through a

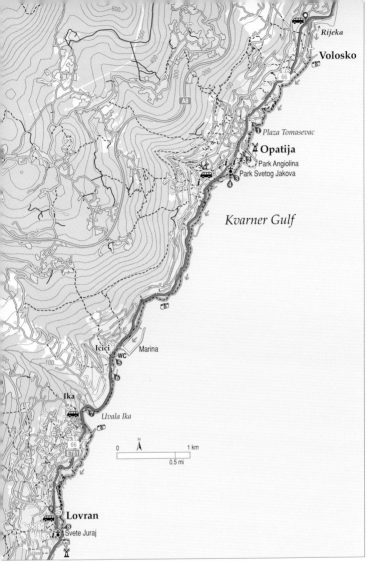

long cloister-like section and soon reach **Ičići** (**❺**; **1h50min**), a port in the Middle Ages and later home to a large Jesuit community. At the far end of the beach the path goes under the main road via **two short tunnels** (**❻**) adorned with murals. Then you come to a wooded stretch leading to sheltered **Ika Bay** (**❼**; **2h10min**), once famous for shipbuilding.

The approach to **Lovran** is lovely, with the sinuous path winding through shade groves. Beside a tall deserted building, go up a path towards restaurants into **Park Bogdana Sirotnjaka Bodija** (**❽**) beyond which is the main road and **bus stops** to the right (**❾**; **2h40min**).

Walk 23 (Kvarner Gulf): LUŽINSKI BREG FROM DOBREĆ

Distance/time: 7km/4.3mi; 2h45min
Grade: ● moderate with 375m/ 1230ft ascent; on quiet minor roads, flights of steps, paths and trails; mostly well waymarked and signposted
Equipment/map: see page 46; walking poles; Učka Nature Park map (1:30,000)
Refreshments: small shop in Dobreć, 100m southeast of bus terminus, open mornings only
Transport: 🚌 From the three-way

junction opposite the tourist office in Lovran, follow Ulica Žrtava Fašizma, then Cesta di Lovransku Dragu, which winds fairly steeply up to a junction where it's right to Dobreć (2.8km). There is an informal car park beside the bus terminus (45° 18.250'N, 14° 15.687'E). Or 🚌 no 36 to Lovranska Draga; alight at Dobreć Centrum where the bus turns to rejoin its main route (see Transport, page 165).
Nearest accommodation: Dobreć (self-catering only), Lovran

This walk provides a not-too-strenuous introduction to the peaks, ridges and forests of Učka Nature Park, with the reward of panoramic views, especially of much of the coast covered by Walk 22 (page 118), as well as Vojak (1396m), the highest peak on the entire Dinaric range. Partly overgrown by the beautiful beech, oak and chestnut forests are the remains of the stone buildings and enclosures of former communities. Depressions and scattered rocky outcrops provide evidence of the local limestone (or karst) landscape. At about the 1h20min mark, near the main route of the walk, is a memorial to a member of the local anti-fascist resistance force who died nearby during World War 2, a poignant reminder that the area was once much less peaceful.

Start the walk from the **bus stop in Dobreć** (●): walk up the road past scattered houses and woodland on the right; within a few minutes turn right along a path to KOZUH ANTICI. This leads to a road which you follow for no more than 100m, past a house on the left, to a forest track. Almost immediately you're following an old stone-paved, stepped path. Soon you pass a house on the right; continue up, passing a sign to KOZUH (and Lovran), climbing fairly steeply.

Beyond some houses keep left at a **junction** (❶) along an old track. Cross a house access road and follow the old track. Within 50m pass a sign to LOVRAN and go

on along a concrete track for 20m to a road, where you turn right (❷; **25min**). The tar then concrete road passes mostly lived-in houses (❸; **Kožuli**) and gains height sharply.

Cross a forest track (**35min**) and go on along an old path to POKLON and GORICA (also Dobreć). Waymarkers now guide you onwards, along an old, well-defined path, comfortably graded. You pass the ruins of a stone house in the trees to the right (**1h10min**). Next you come to a junction with a wide track and signposts, where you could turn sharp left towards LIGANJ (❺). But if you continue ahead for about five more minutes, you will come to the the cairn with

121

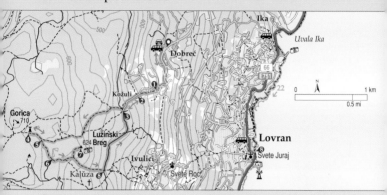

the **memorial plaque** (④) mentioned in the introduction above; it's on the right.

Then return to the main route and bear right for *LIGANJ* (⑤). After about six minutes, bear left at a **fork** (⑥) and within another 10 minutes come to the turn-off for the peak. This is soon followed by another left turn, up a narrow path to the flat, rocky open **Lužinski Breg summit** (⑦; **1h30min**). The extensive view embraces Rijeka, the Opatija-Lovran Riviera and the islands of Cres and Krk out to sea. In early autumn the aromatic perfume of thyme is unmistakeable while a lovely blue-purple thistle-like wildflower (one of the Eryngiums) should be in flower, here and elsewhere.

Return to the junction where you turned off for Lužinski Breg and turn left for Lovran. Descend quite steeply to a track (⑧; **1h50min**); for the most direct return to Dobreć, turn left. On a left bend (**2h10min**) go right and down a steep concrete then bitumen road. Follow this back to the bus stop/car park in **Dobreć** (**2h45min**).

Atop Lužinski Breg

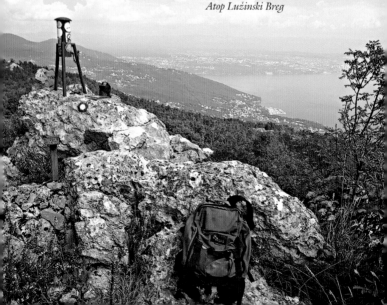

Walk 24 (Kvarner Gulf): VOJAK SUMMIT FROM POKLON

Distance/time: 7.5km/4.7mi; 3h15min

Grade: ● moderate, with 480m/1574ft ascent, on paths, trails and a quiet road; clearly waymarked and signposted

Equipment/map: see page 46; walking poles; Učka Nature Park map (1:30,000)

Refreshments: available daily at Poklon. There are also picnic tables at Poklon and en route (see text).

Transport: 🚌 to Poklon; the following route is slightly less tortuous than that from Ičići. Drive northeast from Lovran on the Rijeka–Pula road (route 66) for about 10km (about 4km from Opatija) and at a junction with a roundabout go left towards *TUNEL*. Go straight on at the next roundabout (where 'Tunel' is to the left). The road then goes underneath the motorway. Turn left at the next major junction, into the town of Matulji ('CENTAR'). Then, just 0.3km further on, take the next left towards *UCKA, VEPRINAC*. At a junction in the village of Mihotići head straight on towards *UCKA*. Continue to Veprinac and a junction with a bar-restaurant and small shop, where you bear right

for *VRANJE* and *UCKA*. Park at Poklon, near the small park office, 26km from Lovran, 22km from Opatija (45° 18.482'N, 14° 12.931'E). Or 🚌 from Opatija to Učka, Sundays only (see Transport page 165). The Opatija bus station is beside the prominent Grand Hotel Palace, about 100m inland from the promenade.

Alternative return loop via the Educational Trail: ● Moderate, just 200m further an 10m/30ft more ascent than the main walk. Follow the main walk to the **Vojak summit** (**❻**) and then back back to the lay-by with picnic table (**❹**). From here follow a wide track up to a crest, then promptly descend. Further on you reach a spectacular **lookout** (**ⓐ**; **1h45min**) close to the cliff edge with a fine view of the summit and the wide valley below. There's another **viewpoint** (**ⓑ**) a little further on. You pass a sign pointing to a **cave** (**ⓒ**; **2h**), then the path bends left and rises above a depression to a picnic table. Here the Educational Trail route bends left; to return to Poklon, go up slightly to join the main route to the left.

T his is the easiest way to reach the summit of Vojak (1396m), if you're prepared for an exciting drive or bus ride to the hamlet of Poklon (922m) sitting on the ancient pass across the ridge crowned by the peak. The bus timetable allows plenty of time to enjoy the summit view, and the beautiful forests en route, then to sample the delights of the restaurant at Poklon. An alternative, slightly longer return route from the summit is described, following an Educational Trail highlighting beech forests, wildlife and limestone formations, and with some superb lookouts.

Start the walk from the far side of the **Poklon car park** (**⓿**) and to the right of the Učka Nature Park office: pass a ring of totem poles

and follow waymarkers up through open forest. After a few minutes, bear right with a sign for Vojak.

Soon, **cross a road** (**❶**)

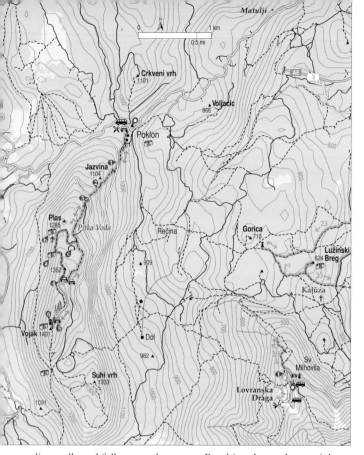

diagonally and follow a path uphill. Turn left at a fork (**10min**) and go up past a low crag, through beech forest. The path then improves markedly, but be vigilant for waymarkers and beware false trails! Shortly turn right at the road and **climb steps** (**❷; 33min**) to the left, then in fairly quick succession go right at a fork, and right and left diagonally across the road. Below the path to the right there's a **picnic table** and **information** about local plants (**❸; 1h**).

Reaching the road, turn right; a little further on you come to a **lay-by** (**❹; 1h17min**) and **picnic table**. *(This is the start of the alternative route back to Poklon.)*

Shortly, on a right bend, go up a path indicated by a red arrow; it returns to the road at **a car park** (**❺**) close to the large communications towers. About 150m further on you come to the **Vojak summit** (**❻; 1h25min**). There's a small souvenir shop inside the prominent **observation tower**

NOTE: The longest cable car in Europe (at 4.7km) is to be built linking Medveja on the coast 2km south of Lovran to Vojak summit (with a substantial contribution from the EU!), due for completion for summer 2021. For more information see www.tz-lovran.hr.

which provides a superb panorama, the features of which are etched around the top of the wall. These include the hotel near Lovranska Draga (see Walk 25, page 126). There's also

information about the history of the tower.

To return to Poklon direct, retrace your steps (**3h15min**), but the alternative return will take hardly any more time.

Ascending to Vojak

Walk 25 (Kvarner Gulf): LOVRANSKA DRAGA

Distance/time: 1.6km/1mi; 30min
Grade: ● easy, with minimal ascent, on signposted minor road and path
Equipment/map: see page 46; walking sandals or shoes suitable; Učka Nature Park map (1:30,000)
Refreshments: Hotel Draga di Lovrana is beside the road in a spectacular location, about 0.5km from the start of the walk in the village centre. Otherwise, available in Lovran
Transport: 🚌 From the three-way junction opposite the tourist office in Lovran, follow Ulica Žrtava Fašizma, then Cesta di Lovransku Dragu, which winds fairly steeply up to a junction where a right turn leads to Dobreć and a left to Lovranska Draga. Continue along the two-way road which shrinks to a narrow single-track road in the village of Tuliševeca. From here beware of oncoming vehicles around the several challenging U-bends. There are a few parking spaces around the start of the walk (45° 16.734'N, 14° 14.627'E). Or 🚌 36 from Lovran to Lovranska Draga; departs from its Lovran terminus in Ulica Žrtava Fašizma, about 100m up from the main road junction in the centre of town. Alight either opposite the start of the walk on a left bend, or at the terminus, so you can walk back through the old village and enjoy the views over the steep-sided valley and out to sea.
Accommodation: Lovranska Draga (hotel), Lovran

Accessible waterfalls in Učka Nature Park are few and this one is regarded as the best — when it's flowing. Therefore try to time your visit to follow a wet day during early spring or mid-late autumn. The short walk also introduces the traditional cultivation and use, dating back to the Middle Ages, of the sweet chestnut (maruni), once widely exported, and still celebrated with a festival during the second half of October. Indeed, the local climate serves to produce a particularly flavoursome chestnut, widely regarded as among the best anywhere. The trees were, and still are to a limited extent, heavily coppiced (regularly cut back), the timber having a variety of agricultural and domestic uses. As the extensive terraces across the slopes of the steep-sided valley show, wine grapes were once cultivated, as were fruit trees, notably cherry. The village occupies a truly spectacular location high above the coast, huddling below soaring cliffs and steep, forested slopes.

The **Šetnica Slap** (Waterfall Path) **starts** at an information board (**❍**) immediately across the bridge on the main/only road. Walk up the minor road, past an **old well**, for about 250m to a sharp left bend with a house access track on the left, to the turnoff to SLAP on the right (**❶**). The trail leads first past terraces of vines then through a beautiful chestnut and hornbeam forest. Soon you cross a **bridge** and gain a little height beside the stream (bed) to a **second bridge**. Nearby a picnic table sits on a flat area, close to the pool below the sheer to overhanging cliff down which the **waterfall** (**❷**) cascades

126

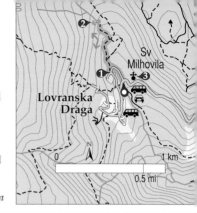

(**15min**). There's an information board here about local wildlife.

Retrace steps to the start (**30min**). I recommend allowing time to walk just 50m up the road to the small baroque **Church of St Michael** (**❸**), open at least on its feast day, 29 September. Through the window you can contemplate the rows of pews and the simple three-part altar.

House and garden in Lovranska Draga

RAB: Introduction

Rab is an attractively compact island and quite small, at least compared with its near neighbours Krk and Cres. Its distinctive features: sandy beaches, woodlands and historic buildings are all easily accessible, as is the highest point on the island, Kamenjack. This summit crowns the long east-west ridge that divides the extensive woodlands on the sheltered southern side from the steep, bare rocky slopes to the north, exposed to the full force of the potentially destructive Bura wind. This is typically a wintertime event and reaches speeds of 200kph and more. The Lopar peninsula is, unusually in the Adriatic, largely composed of sandstone, with several relatively sheltered, safe sandy beaches.

There is an excellent network of marked paths and trails, across the uplands and along the coast. These include an Educational Trail focussed on Rab's status as a potential Geopark, marking its outstanding geological, as well as historical significance. In Rab town, the capital, you will find a fascinating collection of churches and monasteries dating back to medieval times, all beautifully preserved.

Three centres, Rab town, Lopar and San Marino, offer convenient bases for exploring the island, simplified perhaps by the excellent bus services. Rab is accessible from the mainland via Krk or Jablanac on the mainland coast, and from Cres. For more information go to www.rab-visit.com.

Photo: Uvala Dubac and Uvala Podšilo (Walk 26)

Walk 26 (Rab): FROM LOPAR TO SAN MARINO VIA SAHARA BEACH

Distance/time: 7.6km/4.7mi; 2h30min

Grade: ● easy-moderate, with 210m/689ft ascent; on quiet roads, tracks, paths and sandy beaches, following mostly signposted routes

Equipment/map: see page 46; walking shoes suitable; Croatian Mountain Rescue Service map 'Rab Biking and Trekking' (1:25,000)

Refreshments: available at Lopar and San Marino

Transport: 🚌 from Rab town to Lopar (see Transport, page 165); the bus goes to San Marino then to the terminus at Lopar, about 300m south of the ferry terminal. The walk starts at the terminus. Or 🚗

to Lopar: from a junction on the main road above Rab town centre, turn left for Lopar and Traject. About 9km along, on a bend beyond the Zlatni Zalaz turn-off on the left, there's a small lay-by for the view. Some 2km further on, turn left towards Lopar. Continue for 1.1km then turn right along a single-track road signposted to BD MARIJA and PLAZA. There is a small pay car park on the right about 250m along (44° 50.401'N, 14° 43.469'E) and another on the left, a further 500m along. The walk ends at San Marino bus stop, from where drivers can return to Lopar by bus.

Nearest accommodation: Lopar, San Marino, Rab town

Beaches are the magnet for many visitors to Rab, especially those on the Lopar peninsula at its northern end. There is the bonus that all the beaches are sandy (rather than shingle) due to the near universal occurrence of sandstone. Apart from Paradise Beach at the San Marino resort, all the beaches are accessible only on foot. Sahara Beach seems a strange misnomer until you learn that it was so named by visitors in the 1930s, amazed by the extent of people-friendly sand, rather than the shingle common

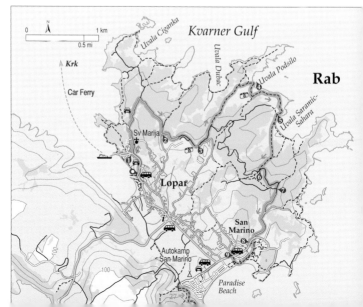

elsewhere. Sahara is designated 'FKK' and is frequented by naturists, but not only naturists. Indeed, Rab and some other islands have been popular with naturists since the 1930s.

The bare white island to the north-east from the beaches featuring on this walk is Goli Otok ('bare island), site of a

Sahara Beach

notorious concentration camp for political prisoners 1949-1956, and for 'normal' prisoners until 1988. It was built using this same sand, also used for house building elsewhere. See Walk 27 overleaf re Rab's potential Geopark, which includes Goli.

A system of waymarked paths brings many of the beaches on the peninsula within walkers' reach. It isn't universally consistent but the following notes should resolve any puzzles and provide a varied exploration of the peninsula.

From the bus terminus at Lopar (**O**) follow the roadside path to the single track road on the right to *BD MARIJA* and *PLAZA* (**❶**; **4min**). Turn right here, passing information about the 14th-century Church of the Blessed Virgin Mary, out of sight in the trees above; it is associated with use of the Glagolitic language (see also Short 'picnic' walk 28, page 44, and Walk 29, page 138). Pass two car parks (**6min, 18min**) then, almost immediately, the turn-off to Ciganka. Stay with this road, past tracks to Sturic and Dubac and another parking area. Just two minutes later, at an unsigned **Y-fork**, turn left (**❷**; **32min**).

This road soon bends right then the tar ends (**37min**). Gain a little more height to an excellent view of the cliff-lined island **Krk**. At the start of more tar (**❸**; **40min**), turn left along the track to *DUBAC*. Some 350m further on, turn left again for *DUBAC* (**45min**). At first the way is rocky but becomes easier further on. At a junction go straight on towards *PODSILO* (**1h**) then, at a fork, head right; a minute later you're on sandy **Podšilo Beach** (**❹**; **1h5min**), complete with an enticing grassy sward.

From here follow the path to the right, signposted to *SAHARA*, and climb easily up to the crest of a small headland, with a lovely view of the three parts of **Uvala Saramić** (Sahara Beach).

The path descends across grass to **Sahara Beach** (**❺**; **1h25min**). About 100m further on, a signpost on a knoll up to the right becomes visible; aim for this to continue quite steeply up into pine woodland. At a gravel track turn sharp left (**❻**; **1h45min**), soon with an excellent view of Sahara opposite. Then you come to a wide path leading up from the left and one opposite; follow the latter up to the right (**1h55min**). After about five minutes you reach a **gravel road** (**❼**; **2h**) with clusters of signposts and information about Sahara Beach.

Turn left towards *SAN MARINO 1.8KM* [referring to the camping ground]. The track eventually becomes a road (**2h15min**). Go down, then at an oblique junction continue to the right, down a quiet road to a T-junction where you go left for *SAN MARINO*. At another T-junction go right for 100m towards *SAN MARINO RESORT* then left (**❽**) on a stone-paved path down to the beach. The bus stop is another five minutes to the right (**❾**; **2h30min**).

Walk 27 (Rab): FROM SAN MARINO TO MATKICI ALONG A GEOTRAIL

Distance/time: 6.6km/4.1mi; 2h10min
Grade: ● easy-moderate with approximately 150m/490ft ascent on minor roads, paths and trails; waymarked and signposted
Equipment/map: see page 46; walking poles; Croatian Mountain Rescue Service map 'Rab Biking and Trekking' (1:25,000)
Refreshments: in San Marino
Transport: 🚗 Drive from Rab town to the roundabout on the edge of Lopar and turn right towards San Marino; turn right again 0.9km further on towards Autokamp San Marino. There is a car park on the right in front of the entrance (44° 49.426'N, 14° 44.228E). Return by 🚐 from the end of the walk near Matkići. Or 🚐 from Rab town to San Marino; alight at the main stop; return on the same bus as above.
Nearest accommodation: Lopar, San Marino, Rab town
Shorter walk: Coastal views; 4km/2.4mi; 1h30min. ● Easy, with 125m/410ft ascent on paths, tracks and trails; equipment transport as main walk. Follow the main walk to the **col** at ❷, then retrace your steps. Superb views of the coast and islands.

This walk ventures onto the open, breezy plateau on the northern reaches of the southeast to northwest ridge extending from one end of Rab to the other. It's a walk of remarkable contrasts, from shady pine forests at the start, through laurel woodlands to the hardy, stunted juniper, cypress and thornbush of the uplands; from the fertile pastures and olive groves of Fruga, to the rocky moonscape of the plateau, exposed to the devastating Bura wind; to the southeast, where it's wooded and sheltered. The wide views embrace nearby islands and mainland mountain ranges. You follow a remarkable, very walker-friendly trail built by forester Ante Premuzik, so look forward to comfortable gradients, both up and down. Rab declared its intention to seek Geopark status in 2008, for its long history, cultural heritage and especially its geological diversity. The walk follows one of the two Educational Geotrails on the island and presents relevant information in distinctive signboards along the way. For more information, go to www.globalgeo park.org and www.rab-visit.com.

Start out from the **main bus stop in San Marino** (❶): walk back beside the road for about 150m; just past **Konzum** on the left, go straight on beside the campground fence to the **Autokamp San Marino** entrance. Continue past cabins on the right to a gate, where you turn left on a cobbled path and cross a small **bridge** (❶; **7min**).

Waymarkers start here, as do information boards, the one here about local geological features and the founder of the trail you're about to follow, Ante Premuzik. The path, with a painted sign for *FRUGA*, curves round to the left (ignore a stony trail heading up right at the outset). This miracle of path design climbs steadily, never steeply, through woodland. Emerging onto the open rocky hillside (**22min**), views of Paradise beach and Goli Otok (see pages 70 and 131) materialise. Dotted about are juniper and stunted cypresses. The path leads up to a **col** (❷; **45min**) and a break in a substantial stone wall on which directions to the left and right are painted; turn left for FRUGA. (*The Shorter walk returns from here.*)

Almost straightaway you discover the **Fruga**'s distinctive landscape: olive groves, grassy meadows and scattered large shady trees. At a subtle **junction** (❸; **53min**), where a track leads to the right, you'll see geological information board no 8 nearby in

Joggers on the Vela Draga path

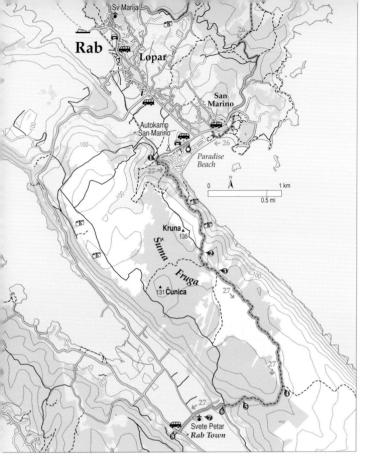

that direction. Turn left for
KAMENJAK, as painted on a rock,
along the waymarked path. Pass a
relatively recent **stone-walled
enclosure** (**1h18min**) and
continue between stone walls.
Ruins of stone buildings on the
slope to the left suggest that there
was once a small settlement here.

The gradual descent down the
steep-sided **Vela Draga** (valley)
soon starts (**1h29min**). At a
junction (**4**) where 'Kamenjak'
is to the left, go straight on. Down at
stream bed level, you encounter
the first of **two retention dams**
(**5**; **1h51min**), built in 1967 as

protection against flash floods (see
also Walk 20, page 112).

Just five minutes later you
reach a **minor road** (**6**); turn
right and follow it round to the left
through right and left bends to a
minor crossroads in **Matkići**. You
can diverge left here to
contemplate the 11th-century
**Benedictine monastery of Svete
Petar** (**7**) and the oldest bell in all
Dalmatia, struck in 1290. The
church is open for mass on
Sundays. Back on the road, it's
only a few minutes to the main
Rab town–Lopar road and the bus
stop (**8**; **2h10min**).

Walk 28 (Rab): KAMENJAK SUMMIT FROM RAB TOWN HARBOUR

Distance/time: 9.3km/5.8mi; 2h45min

Grade: ● moderate, with 408m/ 1338ft ascent; on waymarked and signposted urban and rural paths, trails and quiet roads

Equipment/map: see page 46; walking poles; Croatian Mountain Rescue Service map 'Rab Biking and Trekking' (1:25,000)

Refreshments: in Rab town

Transport: 🚌, 🚐 or ⛴ to Rab town (see Transport, page 165). Park near the head of the harbour (44° 45.578'N, 14° 45.599'E)

Nearest accommodation: Rab town

Shorter walk: Rab town viewpoint; 7.5km/4.5mi; 2h10min. ● Easy-moderate. with 325m/1066ft ascent; equipment and transport as for the main walk. Follow the main walk to **Vidilica Dr M Tomasica** (❸; 1h12min) for fantastic views; retrace steps.

Rab town

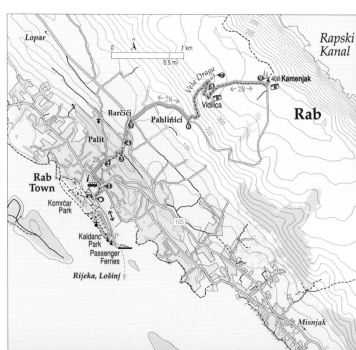

The highest point on an island is an irresistible lure, especially when it's only 408m high, as is Kamenjak on the island of Rab. But this is also an interesting walk in its own right. You start at sea level and walk up through comparatively luxuriant vegetation and past cultivated fields at first, to reach the summit plateau — an utterly different world. The seemingly barren, lunar landscape on the long ridge forming the island's spine, dissected by a maze of stone walls, supports stunted thornbush, prickly juniper and incredibly nimble sheep. The superb view embraces the Učka mountains southwest of Rijeka, the Velebit range to the east, and numerous islands to the south and west.

Start near the southwestern corner of the **small park** (**O**) at the head of **Rab town's harbour**: walk half-right along paved paths through the park, to a road. Ignore the waymarkers leading left along the road (past the bus station); instead, head right towards the roundabout, cross the road and almost immediately turn left (**❶**) along the pedestrian mall. At the far end, just past the fruit and vegetable stalls on the right, turn right along a narrow road, to rejoin the waymarked route through the locality of **Palit**.

Beyond commercial premises and between houses, start to gain height. At a **fork** (**❷**) turn left along a rough track which becomes a cobbled path, winding up the steep hillside. At a **Y-junction** (**❸**) bear left up a concrete track. Turn right at a **minor road** (**❹**) and continue to the main Rab town–Lopar road. Go left to the pedestrian crossing and on to a junction at **Barčići** signposted to *KAMENJAK* (**❺**), where you turn right.

This minor road rises steadily past the scattered houses, fields and olive groves of **Pahlinići** to a junction on the left where a sign points to *KAMENJAK* (**❻**; **42min**).

Follow the path between houses, then gardens, winding uphill and soon bending left into a deep, shady valley. Here you encounter the first of many **gates and barrier**s — too numerous to record here and serving to confine the herds of white sheep. At the head of the valley is a **well** (**❼**; **1h5min**); which will most likely be dry and probably better ignored.

The path changes direction then rises more gently from the next bend. On the edge of the plateau, 20m to the left, is the signposted **Vidilica Dr M Tomasica** 18.10.1932, a circular stone enclosure with a superb panoramic view (**❽**; **1h12min**). *(The Shorter walk turns back here.)*

The path bends left to gain the **plateau** (**1h16min**). Continuing northeast, the path negotiates clumps of thornbush and a mosaic of limestone outcrops — classic karst features (see page 75), and leads to a fenced communications compound on the summit of **Kamenjak** (**❾**; **1h35min**).

To return, retrace your steps via the minor road (**❻**; **2h20min**) and the main road (**❺**; **2h30min**) to the **harbour** at **Rab town** (**2h45min**).

KRK: Introduction

By the slenderest of margins, Krk is the second largest of the Adriatic islands, just behind Cres. Its most prominent landscape features, especially for almost all the walks described here, are the limestone uplands where abundant evidence of traditional sheep grazing survives to this day. The highest point is the bump of Obzova (568m), on the long ridge flanking the southwestern side of the valley above the small town of Baška on the east coast. Across the valley a similar plateau rises to Hlam (461m), dotted with plentiful remains of shepherd's skilfully built stone enclosures. Lower slopes are mostly forested, mainly with pine woodlands, interspersed with pastures. Historical interest resides in the many churches and evidence of the use of the ancient Glagolitic script. The capital is the fine walled town of Krk, settled since Roman times. The base for all but one of the walks is the smaller town of Baška, blessed with an extensive network of waymarked walking routes and a long, if pebbly beach, as well as quiet coves accessible only on foot. There is plenty of variety in the walks described, from Obzova and Hlam on their moonscape plateaus, to the woodlands on the lower slopes. The island is easily accessible, by road bridge southeast of Rijeka and by ferry from the nearby islands of Cres and Rab. For more information go to www.krk.hr.

Photo: on the descent to Rt Škuljica (Walk 32, optional side-trip)

Walk 29 (Krk): ZAKAM, JURANDVOR AND VELA RIKA FROM BAŠKA

Distance/time: 6.7km/4.2mi; 2h25min
Grade: ● easy-moderate, with 200m/650ft overall ascent, on quiet roads, paths, tracks; waymarked and signposted
Equipment: see page 46; walking shoes suitable; Tourist Office of Island Krk map 'Krk Island Mountaineering and Walking Trails' (1:31,500)
Refreshments: available in Baška
Transport: 🚌 or 🚐 to Baška from Krk town (see Transport, page 165). The walk starts and finishes in Baška. Car park by the bus station (44° 58.334'N, 14° 45.340'E)
Nearest accommodation: Baška
Shorter walk: Zakam; 5km/ 3.1mi; 1h24min; ● easy-moderate, with 194m/637ft ascent, on quiet roads, paths, tracks; waymarked and signposted. Equipment and transport as for main walk. Follow the main walk to the **Zakam lookout** (❹; 42min), then retrace steps to Baška.

This is a walk of three distinct parts: a relatively easy ascent to Zakam, an excellent lookout; the walk to an historic church in Jurandvor associated with the Glagolitic tradition (see panel on page 143), and the return along an Educational Trail beside the Vela Rika, the only permanently flowing stream in the Adriatic islands.

St Lucy's Church in Jurandvor was built during the 10th century by Benedictine monks who read and used Glagolitic script. This has survived in the Baška tablet bearing a substantial piece of the script and now kept in Zagreb. Beside the church are the remains of the monastery, abandoned in 1452; the names of the various spaces in an adjacent detailed diagram are in Croatian only. However, printed information in English is available at the nearby visitor centre where guided tours can be arranged.

Baška

Start the walk from the inter-section of Ulica Kralja Zvonimira and Ulica Kralja Tomislava close to the shore in **Baška** (**O**): walk up the latter street, go past the bus station and car park for about 25m and **bear right across a footbridge** (**1**). Walk up the gravel path, cross the main road and continue up a well-graded track to a signpost for ISPOD ZAKAMA (**9min**) then go left at a junction for ZAKAM (**2**).

Beyond a gate continue straight on for ZAKAM and the church (**27min**). The track soon narrows to a path and bends right uphill in an open area. A **vantage point** nearby is good for St John's Church, Baška harbour and Prvic Island against the backdrop of the Velebit range (**35min**).

Continuing on the path, go through a gate; then, in the open, **turn left** (**3**) along a narrow path, as signposted, for about 200m, passing through two stone walls to the informal **Zakam lookout** (**4**; **42min**) at a stone wall: most of Baška's valley, the beach, overlooked by the long ridge from Bag to Obzova, and more distant places are in view. *(The Shorter walk returns to Baška from here.)*

Return to the main path (**3**) ; go through a gate and into pine forest. From another **gate** (**5**; **52min**) the descent to Jurandvor starts, and it's quite steep and rocky at first. Beyond the next gate, the path is flanked by olive groves; then via a cobbled path you reach some houses and a track (**1h23min**). About 20m before

the start of a concrete-surfaced road **turn left** (**⑥**) along a path, the yellow arrow for which, on your right, is not obvious. Cross a bridge and continue beside a stone wall to a gate and steps down to **St Lucy's Church** (**⑦**; **1h33min**). From the church forecourt go down a signposted path and through a small park where the **information centre** is on the right, to a minor road. Turn left then right down to the main road.

Cross straight over and follow a road across a bridge, then turn left as waymarked on a **minor road** (**ⓐ**; **1h41min**) which soon becomes a wide track lined with poplars. Part of an Educational Trail, this follows the channelled course of the **Vela Rika**. After crossing a stream, keep left. At a road on the edge of the village of **Zarok** (**②**; **2h10min**), turn left and follow the roadside path, then the promenade into **Baška** (**2h25min**).

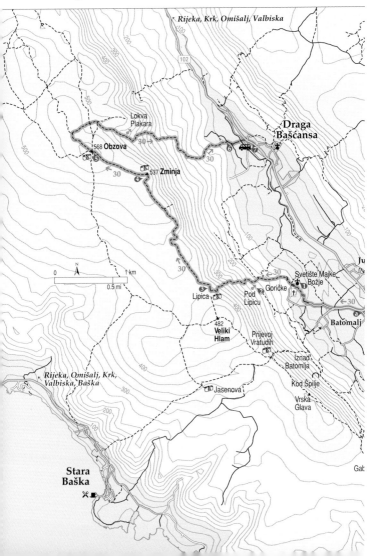

Walk 30 (Krk): OBZOVA SUMMIT FROM BAŠKA

See also photo on pages 138-9
Distance/time: 12km/7.4mi; 4h17min
Grade: ● moderate-strenuous, with 608m/1994ft ascent; on quiet roads, paths, trails and tracks; well waymarked and signposted
Equipment: see page 46; walking poles; Tourist Office of Island Krk map 'Krk Island Mountaineering and Walking Trails' (1:31,500)
Refreshments: available in Baška and Draga Bašćanska
Transport: 🚗 (park as for Walk 29) or 🚌 to Baška, or ⛴ to Valbiska; return on 🚌 from Draga Bašćanska (see Transport, page 165).

Nearest accommodation: Baška
Shorter walks
1 Goričke; 7.6km/4.7mi; 1h15min.
● Easy, with 127m/417ft ascent; walking shoes suitable; transport as for the main walk. Follow the main walk to the Church of the Holy Virgin (**❶**; **Svetište Majke Božje**) at **Goričke** near Batomalj village; retrace steps to Baška.
2 Lipica; 10.6km/6.6mi; 3h40min.
● Moderate, with 400m/1312ft ascent; equipment and transport as for the main walk. Follow the main walk to **Lipica** (**❸**) for panoramic views; retrace steps to Baška.

There's much more to this walk than the ascent of the highest summit on the island, in this case Obzova (568m). Rather than being an independent peak, Obzova is the most elevated point on the long broad ridge enclosing Baška's valley to the west. The walk is also a classic exercise in contrasts, from the oak and pine woodland in the valley to the prickly bushes and wind-pruned pines on the plateau.

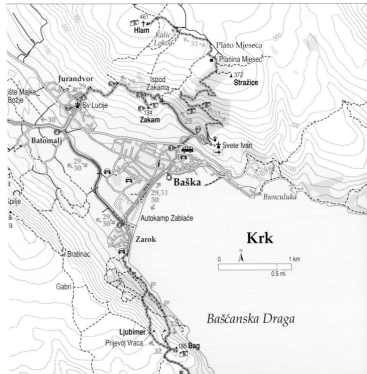

Here the typical karst limestone maze of dissected rock is so pronounced that the gracefully undulating landscape seems to be covered with a whitish glaze or icing.

In the myriad walled enclosures, few of which are still used as pasture or shelter, and deserted stone huts, it is all too easy to see a traditional land use in severe decline — walkers are far more numerous than farmers up here, enjoying this exhilarating, magnificently scenic outing.

Start the walk in the centre of **Baška** (**O**): follow pedestrianised, shoreside Ulica Emila Geistlicha (the founder of tourism in Baška) to a minor road and continue ahead, soon passing a road junction on the right signposted to RIJEKA, with **Autokamp Zablaće** on the left. Walk beside the road to a junction on the right at the village of **Zarok** (**②**; **15min**) and turn right (where there's information about an Educational Trail). Cross a **bridge** and turn right beside a small stream, the **Vela Rika**, the only permanent stream in the Adriatic Islands. Pass a minor road on the left (**25min**); then, at a **T-junction** (**③**), turn left along a road; the village of Jurandvor (Walk 29) is to the right. This quiet road leads to **Batomalj**.

On the edge of the village, at a signposted junction (**27min**) turn right along a minor road towards SV MARIJE. Continue along a track to the right, soon passing a well-maintained **oratory** on the right. Flights of steps then take you up past plaques marking the **Stations of the Cross** to the small 15th-century Church of the Holy Virgin (**Svetište Majke Božje**; **❶**; **45min**) at **Goričke**. Bear right in front of it to reach the entrance and **churchyard**. It may well be open — the paintings, colourful altar and chandeliers are truly beautiful. On the site of a church since the 11th century, this is one of the oldest Marian shrines in Croatia. *(Shorter walk 1 returns from here.)*

From the archway in front of the church, head left then left again towards LIPICA (yellow and white waymarkers). Pass an information board about Folk Architecture in Stone (shepherds' enclosures on the plateau). Go through a gate and at a fork, turn left with the waymarkers. Then ascend at the left of an open area for about 200m and cross it, bearing right. You pass an information board about **Pod Lipicu** (**❷**; a water source) and gain height past a **concrete structure** on the right (**1h5min**). Bear right, through one stone wall and then another; continue up with the waymarkers, soon across some grassland, then in and out of trees with numerous, well-waymarked changes of direction. Pass an excellent **viewpoint** over the valley (**1h20min**).

Cross rocky ground and go on up to a concrete building on the rim of the plateau, with ruined stone enclosures nearby. Continue up, slightly to the right, to a substantial stone wall at a place called **Lipica** (**❸**; **1h40min**). The panorama from here is truly amazing: you look out to the plateau, covered with white limestone 'icing' rising from a cleft below, and to domed Zminja on the skyline beyond stone walls and ruined enclosures. *(Shorter walk 2 turns back here.)*

GLAGOLITIC SCRIPT

The ancient Glagolitic alphabet is a treasured part of Croatia's cultural heritage. It originated in the 9th century when two Greek monks, wishing to convert the Slavic peoples to Christianity, devised a written version of Old Church Slavonic, a language they used at the time. The earliest known examples date from the 11th century and include an inscription in a former Benedictine monastery in Krk town (Walk 33) and the Valun tablet on Cres (Picnic 28). On Krk, there is a replica of a 12th-century carved stone in Svete Lucija church at Jurandvor near Baška (Walk 29). The alphabet was kept alive in Istria and on the islands of the Kvarner Gulf, being used in church documents on Krk until the 19th century. It withstood the spread of the Latin and even enjoyed a short-lived revival during a late 19th-century upsurge of Croatian nationalism, but was doomed by its very nature. Beautifully ornate, its 38 letters comprise intricate loops, scrolls and geometric shapes; it is quite unsuited to rapid inscription! It survives only indirectly, as the antecedent of the Cyrillic alphabet, still used in Serbia and elsewhere.

Photo: Glagolitic inscription at the churchyard near Valun

Now following **red and white waymarkers,** turn right beside the stone wall and cross a dip (**2h**). Take care to follow the change of direction as waymarkers lead right and soon through the stone wall; continue across the fairly feature-less plateau. Bear left past a double circular enclosure, then another on the left and a ruined one on the right. The route drifts right, through a gap in the transverse stone wall, with a gorge below on the right. You then drop steeply to a gate; cross the head of the gully and climb the far side, veering very slightly left over a crumbling stone wall. Walk up the slope, with crags on the left, to less rocky ground and awesome views southeast along the ridge. Continue past a muddy depression, gradually ascending through strange mounds of conglomerate rock. You pass a large grassy enclosure on the left and, bending right, rise to **Zminja** (❹; 537m; **2h45min**). There's a great view of Baška from here.

Descend northwest, through an enclosure, past another on the right, and on past a stand of pines in an enclosure immediately on the left. Then rise past a sunken enclosure to the summit of **Obzova** (❺; 568m; **3h7min**). Among the many features in the panoramic view are the islands of Rab, Goli Otok, Cres and Lošinj, and Krk town.

Following **red and white waymarkers** (rather sparse initially) and a sign painted on a rock (B DRAGA and V LOKI), descend northwest towards a cluster of enclosures below. After about 10 minutes turn left to go through a stone wall, then from a gap in

another wall (where BASKA DRAGA is painted on the wall), walk beside it for about 25m to another gap where DRAGA B and KUNJALABOR indicates a right turn. Descend by the wall and turn right.

From here the path is clear and the red and white waymarkers become easy to follow, down and across a dip. Continue straight on between two enclosures; a narrow path leads right to a **lookout** over the valley. Descend past enclosures, across steep scree beside a low cliff, then down more easily as the valley widens. Bend left on a grassy plateau (**3h34min**). Bear right, away from the valley (**3h56min**), to follow a trail across the slope. Go through a gate (**4h6min**) now descending a wooded spur. After two more gates, at a junction in the open, bear left. Walk down a sloping rock slab to a rocky trail. Meeting an **unsurfaced road** (❻), turn right. Cross a bridge and walk up to the main road in **Draga Baščanska** beside **Kapela Sv Roka** (OBZOVA is painted on the end of its wall); the **bus stop** (❼; **4h 17min**) is about 150m to the right.

View north from Lipica, with one of the many enclosures in the foreground

Walk 31 (Krk): HLAM SUMMIT FROM BAŠKA

Distance/time: 10.5km/6.5mi; 3h20min

Grade: ● moderate, with 461m/1512ft ascent; on quiet roads, paths, trails, tracks; waymarked and signposted

Equipment: see page 46; walking poles; Tourist Office of Island Krk map 'Krk Island Mountaineering and Walking Trails' (1:31,500)

Refreshments: available in Baška

Transport: 🚗 (park as for Walk 29) or 🚌 to Baška, or ⛴ to Valbiska (see Transport, page 165).

Nearest accommodation: Baška

Shorter walks (equipment and transport as for the main walk):

1 Baška view; 4.7km/3mi; 1h15min. ● Easy, with approximately 230m/755ft ascent. Follow main walk to the **viewpoint** at **③** (43min); retrace steps to Baška.

2 Plato Mjeseca; 8km/5mi; 2h10min. ● Easy-moderate, with 370m/1215ft ascent. Follow the

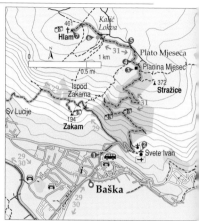

main walk to the T-junction at **⑤** (just past **Plato Mjeseca**). Then retrace steps to Baška. (This is an easier descent than the much steeper, yellow-waymarked trail from near Plato Mjeseca, and you'll find that it's a completely different experience from the ascent.)

The local name for the greater part of this walk, 'Put ka Mjesecu' (Moon Way), isn't inappropriate. It takes you from near the prominent and historic church of St John (Crkva Svete Ivan) up to the plateau on the eastern side of Baška's valley via a superbly graded trail. The rolling uplands are greener than those of the ridge to the west, and there are even a few clumps of trees, together with the characteristic stone walls and circular enclosures. The dense mosaic of fractured limestone nonetheless confers a whitish, washed-out appearance to the landscape. As ever, the panoramic views are seemingly limitless en route to and from the summit of Hlam (461m), proving that you don't need to climb high for the best vistas.

Start the walk from the intersection of Ulica Kralja Zvonimira and Ulica Kralja Tomislava in **Baška** (**○**): walk up the latter street, past the bus station and car park for about 25m, then **bear right across a footbridge** (**①**). Go up the gravel path and cross the main road. Continue up to another road and turn right. Follow this

winding road to **Svete Ivan** (**②**; **19min**), the first parish church in the valley. It dates from the 11th century, is dedicated to St John the Baptist and open daily during the morning June-September. In the large cemetery some family plots date back to the 19th century.

From the entrance to the church grounds follow the blue

Trail near the viewpoint past the U-bend

and white waymarked trail up past a ruined **chapel**, through a gateway and into pines. Of the several benches along the way, some afford fine views; those at the 38min-mark and especially the **viewpoint** (**3**) at the 43min-mark on top of a small crag, are superb. *(Shorter walk 1 returns from here.)*

Beyond a U-bend, there's a new view — of Bunculuka Bay and the island of Prvic. Passing through more stunted, sparser pines, you reach the plateau and

then a timber shelter on the left at **Plato Mjeseca** (**4**; **1h12min**), with information about a local Ornithological Reserve (see the Beli Visitor Centre, see Car tour 9, itinerary 2, page 28) and the impact of sheep grazing on the landscape. Go through a gap in the nearby stone wall and along a narrow path, to a **T-junction** (**5**). Turn right here. *(This is where Shorter walk 2 turns back.)*

Follow **blue waymarkers** around some enclosures, through a gap in a stone wall and to an unsurfaced road (**1h17min**). Turn left to a nearby gate, then follow the **path beside the stone wall** (**6**) on the left, soon veering away from it. Follow waymarkers very carefully past clusters of stone-walled enclosures. Dip down to skirt **Kalić Lokva** (**7**; **1h25min**), a small pond, then gain height and follow cairns and waymarkers to a clear path. This leads to a gate in the stone wall. Continue beside the wall, diverging from it to reach the summit cairn and cross on **Hlam** (**8**; **1h37min**). The panoramic view is incredible, from the Učka mountain range, to Rijeka, the town of Senj and the Velebit mountains beyond, the islands of Pag, Rab, Lošinj and Cres, not to mention local features.

Return the same way to **Baška** (**3h20min**). Take care beyond the double gate to turn right through the stone wall and continue to **Plato Mjeseca** (**4**) and onwards. On the way down from St John's church there's a good example of seeing things differently as you retrace steps. Just above the U-bend below the church there is a sign on the ground next to a bit of stone wall, about Baška castle and the beginning of settlement at Baška in the 13th century.

Walk 32 (Krk): BAG SUMMIT FROM BAŠKA, WITH OPTIONAL DETOUR TO RT ŠKULJIKA

Distance/time: 5.3km/3.3mi; 2h5min

Grade: ● easy-moderate, with 255m/836ft ascent; on waymarked and signposted quiet roads, trails and paths

Equipment/map: see page 46; walking poles, swimming things; Tourist Office of Island Krk map 'Krk Island Mountaineering and Walking Trails' (1:31,500)

Refreshments: Zarok and Baška

Transport: 🚌 or 🚐 to Baška, or ⛴ to Valbiska (see Transport, page 165). There is a pay car park on the right in Zarok at the end of the road (44° 57.626'N, 14° 44.803'E).

Nearest accommodation: Baška

Shorter walk: See Picnic 24, page 43

Extension, Rt Škuljica: See overleaf

Looking out to sea from Baška's promenade to the rugged, cliff-encrusted headland on the western side of the bay, you'd scarcely credit that there's an easy route up to the ridge. This walk removes all such doubts — there's a skilfully routed path across the cliff faces, with a slight hint of exposure. A short climb to the small peak of Bag affords superb views, and the return along the ridge, carpeted with wild sage in springtime, is a sensory delight. A strongly recommended, optional side-trip takes you to a tiny secluded beach and to the nearby beacon on Rt Škuljica. This is a wonderful vantage point from which to contemplate the spectacular bare cliffs and long sweeping ridges on the island of Prvic just across the water, which in their magnificently colourful splendour fill the view seawards from Baška at sunset.

Start from the road junction near the entrance to **Autokamp Zablaće** (◯; 0.5km south of the centre of **Baška**): walk along the roadside path, then the road, to the modern village of **Zarok** at the western end of the bay. Beyond the end of the tar, go part-way across a small open area; bear right up a **trail with a signpost** (❶) to

Baška from Bag summit

1h5min), for fine views of the islands of Prvic (nearby), Rab and Lošinj, the Baška valley and the Velebit range on the mainland.

Return to **Prijevoj Vraca**, from where you can make an optional, highly recommended, side trip to Rt Škuljica (see below). To continue the main walk, follow **blue waymarkers** up the slope, to the inconspicuous summit of **Ljubimer** and on to the adjacent saddle (**7**; **1h21min**), where BAŠKA is painted in green on a gap in the stone wall. Descend into a small valley; this **green-waymarked** route soon swings left across the slope, past cliffs and the steep, rock-encrusted mountainside, losing height steadily. Go through an old gate in a stone wall (**1h36min**) and descend through pines. Go through another stone wall and downhill a short distance. When you rejoin your outgoing path at **2** (**1h41min**), retrace your steps to **Baška** (**2h5min**).

Optional side-trip to Rt Škuljica (add 3km/1.8mi; 1h; 150m/492ft ascent). From **Vraca** follow the **yellow waymarked route** downhill along a path beside the stone wall, into a wide valley. Bend left at the corner of the wall and descend a stream bed and then a path. Pass the head of a **deep cleft** (**a**) where it's easy to imagine that one day the land ahead will become an island. Soon you come to a tiny sheltered beach with a flight of steps into the water from where it's only a short step on a clear path across the slope to the **beacon** (**b**; **27min**) at **Rt Škuljica**. There's a great view northeast to the mainland and the Velebit mountains, and across the narrow strait to the island of Prvic. Retrace your steps to **Vraca** (**1h**).

various destinations and information about sand mining here. Cross an open space and follow a wide path. Soon it bends left and overlooks the bay. Cross a dip (**20min**) and follow the path along the rim of the low cliff. Pass a junction with a **green-waymarked path** (**2**; **28min**), your return route.

After a narrow, faintly exposed stretch of no more than 100m, the **path bends right** (**3**), up into a pine forest, and meets a path beside a **stone wall** (**4**; **34min**) — a first setting for Picnic 24. Turn left here. On the far side of a gate (**36min**; a second setting for Picnic 24), a rockier path leads up towards seemingly impenetrable cliffs. Follow a broad rock ledge into a valley and climb steeply to **Prijevoj Vraca** (**5**; **56min**), the saddle on the main ridge enclosing Baška's valley to the west.

From here follow the clearly waymarked route up beside a stone wall initially. Then head left, up to the summit of **Bag** (**6**; 185m;

Walk 33 (Krk): PRNIBA POINT FROM THE KRK CAMPING RESORT ACCESS ROAD

Distance/time: 7.6km/4.7mi; 2h15min

Grade: ● easy, with approximately 90m/295ft ascent on unsurfaced roads signposted for cycle routes

Equipment/map: see page 46; walking shoes or sandals suitable; swimming things; Tourist Office of Island Krk map 'Krk Island Mountaineering and Walking Trails' (1:31,500)

Refreshments: in Krk town

Transport: 🚌 or 🚐 to Baška, or 🛥 to Valbiska (see Transport, page 165). *Travelling by car:* from the Krk town–Baška road, the turn-off to the start of the walk is about 50m past a petrol station and signed to Krk Camping Resort. Parking is available before this junction on the right, either at Crkva Sv Lucija (St Lucy's Chapel) or nearby, about 50m before the turnoff (15° 1.764'N, 14° 35.167'E). *On foot from Krk town (1.7km/1mi each way):*

from the bus station walk through the old walled town, exiting via the eastern (13th-century Pizan) gate. Bear right along Ulica Puntarska, cross Ulica Ružmarinska to Ulica Vlade Tomašića, then take the first left (Ulica Dubašljanska) and the third right (Ulica Omišaljska). This brings you to the main road: turn right for 200m, past Sv Lucija, to a road informally signed *KRK CAMPING RESORT*.

Nearest accommodation: Krk town

Shorter walk: Two bays; 5.5km/ 3.4mi; 1h20min. ● Easy, with approximately 70m/230ft ascent; equipment and transport as for the main walk. Follow the main walk to ❸ (**23min**); turn right and continue to a T-junction (**33min**); turn right and follow the main walk from the 1h17min-mark, past **Uvala Valunta** and **Uvala Svete Danijel**, back to the start.

Τhe setting for this walk— the largely pine-clad peninsula on the northeastern shore of Krčki Zaljev, east of Krk town — is markedly different from Baška's valley and ridges. The peninsula was once intensively cultivated, as the intricate pattern of stone walls and trails illustrates. Only a few small

Uvala Valunta

fields are still cultivated, mainly with olive groves. Some of the old trails have been widened and transformed into unsurfaced roads. There are a few faded red and white waymarks here and there; signposting is for Cycle Routes 6, 6.1 and 6.2, just as relevant for walkers. There are pleasant views of the bay, Puntarska Draga, from two vantage points, and secluded coves on the south coast for a swim.

Start along the road signposted to KRK CAMPING RESORT (**O**). Follow this for just 350m, to a right bend, then turn left along a road signposted for CYCLE ROUTES 6, 6.1 and 6.2 (**1**). You will return from the right later. The road shortly becomes unsurfaced. Keep left at a junction on the right (**2**; **18min**). At the next junction, a left turn would take you the short distance to the peaceful shore of Puntarska Draga, but keep ahead here, ignoring a road to the right (Cyclists Route 6.2; **23min**). *(But for the Shorter walk turn right here.)*

Ignore a second road to the right (**5**); continue to the long stone **jetty at Puntarska Draga** (**4**), with small Otok Košljun close by and the marinas and houses of the small town of Punat beyond. The pine-shaded shingle cove close is ideal for a picnic (**33min**).

Retrace your steps and turn left at the **first junction** (**5**). The unsurfaced road crosses a low hill then descends, past a road on the right (**6**). When it ends 300m

further on (**58min**), continue through the pines for about 75m, to the rocky shore at **Prniba Point** (**7**), overlooking the narrow entrance to Puntarska Draga.

Return along the road and take the first left turn (**6**; CYCLISTS ROUTE 6; **1h5min**); pass a road on the right (**1h17min**). *(The Shorter walk rejoins here.)* Soon, **Uvala Valunta** is worth a pause, as is a nameless cove further on (**1h27min**). **Uvala Svete Danijel** (**1h34min**), though more open, is no less attractive. Continue with the cyclists past screened FKK beach **Politin** (**8**; **1h44min**). At the far end turn right, still with the cyclists, and continue up to a **T-junction** (**9**) marked with a sign to NATURIST BEACH. Turn left and you soon reach Krk Camping Resort's boundary fence. Continue to the start at the access road, where Sv Lucija is nearby to the left (**2h15min**). Then, if you came by bus, retrace your steps to the bus station in Krk town (allow about 25 minutes).

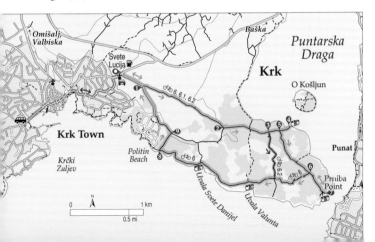

LOŠINJ: *Introduction*

Lošinj is linked to Cres and the historic village of Osor by a bridge across a channel cut in Roman times, making a two-island visit the natural choice. It is similarly long (33km) and even more slender than Cres — from almost 5km down to just 250m. The elongated Osoršćica ridge, crowned by the accessible summit Televrin (586m) dominates the northern half; the southern half's profile is lower and is where you'll find the neighbouring towns of Mali Lošinj, now about four times the size of Veli Lošinj. Lošinj's historical interest lies mainly in Roman remains; in churches, large and small; in the old walled village of Osor (actually in Cres, but in the context of this book, just as relevant to Lošinj); and in its maritime history — Mali Lošinj was once a major Adriatic port. The island is blessed with a rich biodiversity and much-indented coastline. Walkers are generously catered for, from the popular summit of Televrin to paths between the two towns and beyond, and to remote and beautiful coves and beaches where you can easily combine walking and swimming.

For more information go to www.visitlosinj.hr

Photo: fishing nets drying at Osor

Walk 34 (Lošinj): FROM NEREZINE TO OSOR VIA THE TELEVRIN SUMMIT

Distance/time: 13.6km/8.4mi; 4h55min

Grade: ● moderate with approximately 640m/2099ft ascent; on quiet roads, trails and paths; well waymarked and signposted

Equipment/map: see page 46; walking poles; Mali Lošinj Tourist Board leaflet (1:20,000)

Refreshments: Nerezine and Osor

Transport: See page 165: 🚌, 🚢 or 🚐 to Cres or Lošinj. Then ideally, early bus to Nerezine, mid-afternoon return from Osor. *NB: the bus timetable may also be compatible with a start from Cres town.* At Nerezine the bus shelter is about 8 minutes' walk north of the trail's starting point. The bus stop at Osor is on Cres, 50m northeast of the bridge over the channel. Travelling by 🚗 is of course timetable dependant: drive to Osor, cross the bridge and turn left to a car park (44° 41.601'N, 14° 23.499'E) or continue a short distance to more space on the right beyond the marina. Return to Nerezine by a convenient bus.

Nearest accommodation: Mali Lošinj, Veli Lošinj, Cres town

Shorter walk: Počivalice; 5.6km/ 3.5mi, 2h20min. ● Moderate, with 246m/807ft of ascent; equipment and transport as for the main walk. Follow the main walk to **Počivalice** (**❺**; 1h10min), then retrace your steps to Nerezine.

Shorter walk: Dom Sv Gaudent; See Walk 35 on page 155.

This popular walk takes you to Televrin; at 586m, it's the highest point on the long Osoršćica ridge at the northern end of Lošinj, a dominant feature in views northwards from Mali Lošinj. There is a short section with a fixed cable (beyond the summit), but it is definitely *not* exposed or difficult. As a very scenic linear walk, it *can* be done in either direction. But the description below, from south to north, has a more convenient finish in the village of Osor, on the main road. Take time to inspect the collection of bronze statues on a musical theme (the long-standing Osor classical music festival takes place annually, July-August), standing around the prominent 15th-century church of Svete Gaudenico; the nearby archaeological museum, with a collection of Roman artefacts, might just be open. The route described here is the longer of two from Nezerine. The other, following a route signposted to Svete Nikola from near the bus stop is more direct but much steeper.

Start the walk from the **bus shelter** in **Nerezine** (**O**): walk back along the road, past the lane signposted to Svete Nikola (**❶**), to a minor road signed to *PODGORA* and *SV MIKUL* where you turn right (**❷**; **8min**). At a fork beside a house (3 Podgora) turn left with waymarkers, then left again at a prominently marked path which crosses the main road via an underpass. On the far side, go right along a path in a channel; almost at its end, turn **left uphill** (**❸**). As you climb there's a good view across the hillside (**43min**) which you soon cross though pines and juniper.

Having reached the south side of the crest (**1h**), continue up steeply past a **junction to Vela Jama** (cave; **❹**). The next staging point is the subsidiary summit of **Počivalice** (**❺**; 246m/807ft; **1h 10min**), complete with a visitors' book in a metal box. The inshore island to the west is Unije. *(The Shorter walk returns from here.)*

Bear right through a pine grove then up across boulders following a clearly marked line, soon into scattered pines and still gaining height. The gradient eases beside a stone wall; go through it then across a dip (**1h45min**). Then more boulders lead to an open knoll, from where a good deal more of the same takes you up to **Svete Mikul/Nikola** (**❻**; **2h 30min**) with a fine view north-wards along the ridge .

With the chapel on your left

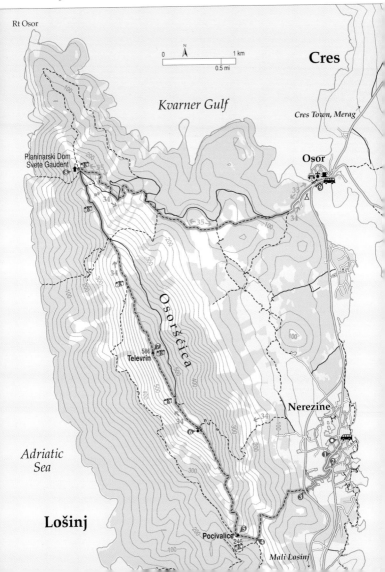

Osor village setting from the summit of Televrin

continue down on a good path, past the **junction** with the direct route from Nerezine. Cross a dip, with colourful views of the inshore waters. In an open area with antennas (**2h47min**) and signs to caves on the left and right, follow the vehicle track for about 80m then turn left with waymarkers to **Televrin summit** (**7**; **3h9min**) and its cairn, which you reach via a narrow path and short rocky stretch. A little further on, Osor comes into view encouragingly.

The path crosses to the western side of the ridge and the going underfoot becomes easier. Then you come to the firmly anchored, 50m-long cable across the low cliffs (**3h30min**). Soon the

surroundings change dramatically as you emerge onto an open plateau. Pass a large **cairn** (**3h50min**) then another about 200m further on to reach a vehicle track where **Planinarski Dom Svete Gaudent** (**8**; **4h10min**; see Walk 35 opposite) is to the left. Cross the road and follow a waymarked path down through pleasant woodland, often with a feet-friendly surface. At a path junction bear right, along the path from Planinarski Dom (**4h35min**). Continue down the waymarked path, occasionally touching on the track. When the path ends, follow the track down through the camp ground, to the main road/**bus stop** at **Osor** (**9**; **4h55min**).

Walk 35 (Lošinj): PLANINARSKI DOM SVETE GAUDENT FROM OSOR

Distance/time: 9.6km/6mi; 3h
Grade: ● easy-moderate, with 360m/1181ft ascent; on unsurfaced roads, trails and paths; signposted and waymarked
Equipment: see page 46; walking poles; Mali Lošinj Tourist Board leaflet (1:20,000)
Refreshments: at Osor and at Planinarski Dom at least on week-ends during spring and autumn and daily during July and August
Transport: See page 165: 🚗, 🚢 or 🚌 to Cres, or 🚢 to Lošinj. Then mid-morning 🚌 from Veli/

Mali Lošinj to Osor (on Cres). Return by the mid/late afternoon 🚌 from Osor to Mali/Veli Lošinj. *NB: the bus timetable is also compatible with a start from Cres town.* The bus stop at Osor is on Cres, 50m northeast of the bridge over the channel. Travelling by 🚗, drive to Osor: cross the bridge and turn left immediately to a car park (44° 41.601'N, 14° 23.499'E) or continue to more space on the right just beyond the marina.
Nearest accommodation: Mali Lošinj, Veli Lošinj, Cres town

The Osorščica ridge is one of the highlights of walking throughout the Adriatic islands — high, open, and exceptionally scenic, with fine views north and westwards. Walk 34 describes a fairly lengthy traverse; this walk intro-duces the ridge and provides the opportunity to visit a superbly sited mountain hut at the northern extremity of the ridge. Plan your visit so that you can enjoy suitable refresh-ments when you arrive; later, back in Osor, it's well worth allowing some time to inspect the collection of bronze

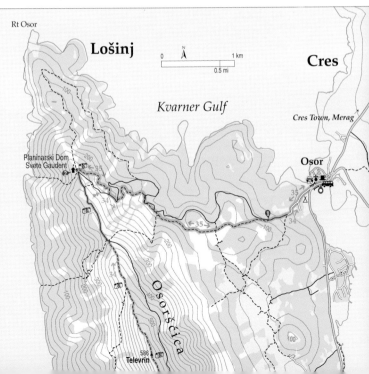

sculptures standing around the prominent 15th-century church of Svete Gaudenico. With luck, the nearby archaeological museum, with a collection of Roman artefacts, might just be open.

Start the walk at **Osor** (**0**): cross the **bridge over the channel** between Cres and Lošinj and turn right at the entrance to the **camping ground**, where there is information about Svete Gaudenica (a medieval bishop of Osor) and Osorščica. Walk up the unsurfaced, waymarked road to the signposted turn-off to PLANINARSKI DOM (**1**; **12min**) and turn left.

The route to the Dom is along a chain of mainly woodland paths, crossing a vehicle track in a few places and following it only briefly to ensure that you take the most direct route. Each crossing is well waymarked. Ignore signposted junctions to other destinations leading left or right, and go on up

to a gate in front of the **Dom** (**2**; **1h30min**).

There are shaded benches and plenty of vantage points for the wonderful view which embraces the islands of Pag, Rab (see pages 128-136), Krk (pages 137-150), Unije, and nearby Sis on Cres (Short 'picnic' walk 30, page 44), the Velebit range on the mainland to the east and Istria and the Učka

range (Walk 24, page 123) to the north.

To return to **Osor**, retrace your steps (**3h**).

Planinarski Dom Svete Gaudent

Walk 36 (Lošinj): ACROSS THE ISLAND'S SPINE

Distance/time: 13.6km/8.4mi; 3h55min
Grade: ● moderate, with approximately 450m/1476ft ascent; on roads, unsurfaced roads, trails and paths, waymarked and signposted
Equipment/map: see page 46; walking poles, swimming things; Mali Lošinj Tourist Board leaflet (1:20,000)
Refreshments: available at Veli Lošinj and the Konoba Balvanida
Transport: See page 165: 🚌 to Lošinj. Or 🚗, 🚌 or 🚐 from Rijeka to Cres and Mali-Veli Lošinj

Nearest accommodation: Veli Lošinj, Mali Lošinj
Shorter walk: Svete Nikola; 6.7km/4mi; 1h45min. ● Easy, with approximately 80m/262ft ascent; equipment and transport as for the main walk. Follow the main walk to **Svete Nikola** (**④**; 1h26min). Walk down the narrow road to a flight of steps, cross the large car park, pass the bus stop on the right and then another car park. At a roundabout, turn right or left to Veli Lošinj harbour.

Very many of the walks in this book make use of old trails and paths built by local people as they went about their daily lives, but this one is different. It follows paths built along the eastern shore of Lošinj for the health and well-being of visitors and residents, thanks to the enthusiasm of wealthy German patrons. The walk takes you across the island's spine to a delightful restaurant (Konoba Balvanida), and to some enticing sheltered coves on the west coast. The historical theme returns for the closing stages as you descend a 200-year-old trail built for Napoleon's troops.

Set out along the eastern side of the **harbour** at Veli Lošinj (**O**) and soon climb steps below the imposing church of Svete Antun built in 1774 and with a magnificent Baroque interior. Coming up to a concrete path, follow it (Picnic 26) past a **chapel** built by Italian craftsmen in the 19th century and down to a terrace beside a **beacon** at the harbour entrance. Bear right along a path, through the archway of the Italianate '**Rotonda**' above.

When you come to a **fork** (**❶**), bear left and downhill, to walk past restaurants and around tranquil **Rovenska harbour** (**18min**). This path between Rovenska and Javorna was built in 1897 at the behest of Baron Carl Püttlingen. Continue past another restaurant and a small shingle beach to a long

breakwater. This was built in the mid-19th century, linking a tiny island to the mainland, to provide protection from southerly and easterly winds, in the hope that a ship-building industry could develop, but only a few vessels were built. Beyond a small point, the firm surface comes to an end between two small coves; continue along the trail on the right-hand side of the stone wall, to **Uvala Javorna** (**❷**; **42min**).

Through much wilder, more remote coastal scenery, you come to a large cove called **Kriška**; a plaque here reminds passers-by of the work of Richard Haasis in sponsoring a coast path in 1911-1912. It's then a short step to a signposted **junction** (**❸**; **1h4min**), where you bear right for SV NIKOLA. Follow the red and blue

157

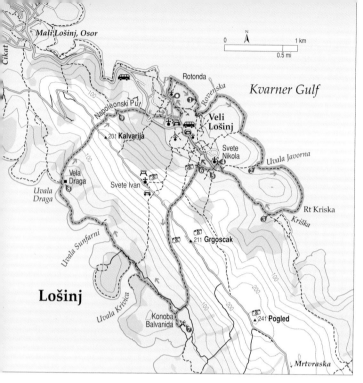

waymarked path; it climbs, with a few interruptions, past terraces and olive groves, and up steps to **Svete Nikola** (❹; **1h26min**), the oldest church in Veli Lošinj, dating from about 1400, also known as Svete Ana. Marking the beginning of settlement in the area, it is open on

Svete Ana day, 26th June. *(The Shorter walk returns from here.)*

Onward directions are painted on a stone wall roughly opposite the church; continue to the right, along a path between stone walls. Shortly, at a **T-junction** (**⑤**), turn right, then soon left at **another 'T'** (**⑥**) towards BALVANIDA. Another 10 minutes of ascent, plus left and right turns, bring you to the road across the plateau (**1h50min**; see Car tour 8, Itinerary 3, page 30). Cross straight over the road and continue on a waymarked trail towards KONOBA BALVANIDA. The trail descends across the open slope, with great views of Krivica inlet below.

At a broad stony clearing with a junction, turn right for BALVANIDA for 50m; continue straight on and down to a better track. Soon, go through a gate to cross a small field and you've arrived at the homely **Konoba Balvanida** (**⑦**; **2h20min**) and its shaded verandah, the epitome of tranquillity. Fish is on the menu

(of course), or you can enjoy a long cold drink.

Rejoin the main route at the junction where you turned left to Balvanida and go straight on towards KRIVICA. After a few minutes, follow a path beside a white-gravelled track via flat, sheltered and shady **Uvala Krivica** (**2h35min**) — a popular anchorage and a fine place for picnics — to the shingle beach at **Uvala Sunfari**. Make your way along the shoreline rocks, across a small beach and more rocks then turn right into the trees. The path crosses a headland and leads to **Vela Draga** (**⑧**; **3h7min**), where there is a large white building beside a path junction.

From here a rocky trail takes you inland, on and between stone walls, to a junction (**3h20min**). Continue straight up an easier path to the road near a small **summit** (**3h27min**). Cross the road to follow the stony trail, once known as **Napoleonski Put** and signposted to VELI LOSINJ. This trail has clearly deteriorated since his day, but soon improves and leads to a **junction** (**⑨**; **3h37min**). Turn right for VELI LOSINJ (or left for MALI LOSINJ) and continue down to the main road and a parking area. Cross the road; 30m to the right, go down a path, through a car park and follow the path signed to MARINE EDUCATION CENTRE and **Veli Lošinj harbour** (**3h55min**).

Veli Lošinj harbour and the church of Svete Antun, where the walk begins

CRES: Introduction

Sitting between the mainland and island Krk, Cres is the largest of the Adriatic islands. The northern part is long and slender while in the south it's broader and almost joined to Lošinj. The island is sparsely populated, hilly rather than mountainous, and the mainly cliff-lined coast is an endlessly fascinating ring of inlets, bays and tiny coves. Cres is of immense natural value, with a high degree of biodiversity, and is part of the Europe-wide Natura 2000 network of protected areas. In the north are dense oak forests; the central section is typified by open rocky pastures, partly overgrown with juniper; in the south the pastoral landscape is a mosaic of stone walls. The highest point is centrally situated Gorice (648m) just topping the adjacent summit of Sis (see Short 'picnic' walk 30, page 44).

Cres was first settled around 1500 BC. Later, the Romans built roads to connect small settlements; the long-lasting rule of the Venetians from the early 15th century is still in evidence, in the excellent museum in Osor, at its southern extremity beside the bridge to Lošinj, and particularly in the capital Cres town. This low-key, relatively quiet small town has an old world feel, and is the ideal base for exploring the island. The walks featured here focus on local history, the coast, huge vistas, while never forgetting places to swim.

Cres is easily accessible from Brestova on the mainland to Porozina in northwestern corner, or from Krk via Valbiska to Merag on the eastern side.

For more information go to www.tzg-cres.hr.

Photo: olives groves spread far and wide beyond stone walls (Walk 37)

Walk 37 (Cres): SVETE SALVATUR AND GAVZA

Distance/time: 8km/4.9mi; 2h35min
Grade: ● easy, with 150m/492ft ascent; along paths, a quiet road, trails; waymarked and signposted down to Uvala Gavza
Equipment/map: see page 46; walking shoes suitable; Geodetski zavod Slovenije, Kvarner road map (1:100,000)
Refreshments: available in Cres town and along the promenade

Transport: 🚌, ⛴ or 🚐 to Cres (see Transport, page 165)
Nearest accommodation: Cres town
Alternative walk: to Svete Salvatur and return: 8km/4.8mi; 2h20min. ● Easy, with approximately 150m/492ft ascent; equipment and transport as for the main walk. Follow the main walk to **Svete Salvatur** (**❻**; 1h10min) then retrace steps to Cres harbour.

The cultivation of olives and the production of fine oils has a long and continuing history on Cres; indeed a bottle of the local extra virgin oil, dark golden-green, with an unusual flavour, is as good a memento of the island as you could wish. This walk takes you through some of the extensive groves on the hillsides north of the town. On the outskirts you will pass a tall round tower, recently restored

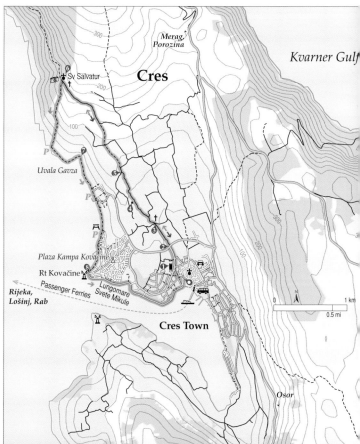

and open for inspection daily. It dates from the 16th century when the ruling Venetians built a wall to enclose the town during their long ascendancy, almost unbroken from 1000 to 1797. Three gates, a fragment of the wall and this tower are the sole surviving remnants of the fortification. The return from Svete Salvatur leads down to tiny Uvala Gavza and the start of the long shoreline promenade to Cres harbour, with many opportunities for a swim.

Start out at the head of **Cres harbour** (**O**), at the corner of Palada on the left. Walk up the shallow steps of Rialto to an intersection. Turn right along Zagrebačka Ulica, to a T-junction and bear right. Continue past the **Venetian tower** (**1**) to another T-junction and bear diagonally right across the road to a signposted trail (**2**; **10min**).

The wide cobbled trail is flanked by stone walls beyond which olive groves spread far and wide. Follow the trail for 350m to a gate, beyond which you go

noticeably now, go through an intersection (**42min**). A few minutes further on part of Cres town comes into view. There's no change of direction at the next intersection as the track bends left and more of Cres town appears. Pass a **large shrine** on the left, flanked by two agaves; then the track levels out to the chapel in honour of **Svete Salvatur** (**❻**; **1h10min**).

Although the plaque over the door is dated 1857, the church is much older and is still used. Through small windows in the doors you can appreciate the discreetly colourful interior. Prominent in the wonderfully wide views across the sea are the coast of Istria to the west and the village of Valun, at the head of its long bay, to the south (see Picnic 28, page 44).

Go down to the left opposite the chapel entrance, as indicated by a sign on a stone wall, CRES VIA GAVZA. The path is rocky at first then earth- and gravel-surfaced as it wanders through pines, then olive groves, gently downhill. It soon steepens to descend between stone walls to the **shore** (**1h35min**). Turn left and in 10 minutes come to **Uvala Gavza** (**❼**; **1h45min**). Cross the upper edge of the shingle to reach steps and the start of a concrete path. Pass the entrance to **Camping Kovačine** (**2h5min**) and a section of the shore designated FKK/ naturist, then curve round **Rt Kovačine** (**❽**) and continue to **Cres harbour** (**2h35min**).

straight over a crossing track and continue ahead on a **wider track** (**❸**). Shortly, pass a small **shrine** on the left and a **wooden cross**, the first of several devotional features along the way. Then a sign welcomes you to an **area of centuries-old olive groves.**

You pass a ruinous **stone building** on the left (**❹**; **25min**). Almost immediately, continue straight on as signposted. At a **gravel track** (**❺**; **33min**) turn right along an easier track (as indicated on the stone wall). Soon, go straight ahead at the next junction. Gaining height

For **ferry information, timetables and reservations** on overnight journeys, see the website of the main provider: Jadrolinija (www. jadrolinija.hr). Websites for other ferry companies are given below. Timetables are usually available from local tourist information offices and are always posted outside local offices. Summer timetables generally operate from late May to early Oct; outside the 'season' services are less frequent and some don't run at all.

For **bus timetables** and more information, see the operator's website: all have English versions unless noted. For journeys on popular routes (Split–Dubrovnik, Split–Rijeka, Zadar/Split–Plitvice Lakes), it is essential to book ahead, either via a company website or by using one of the general ticketing sites, such as www.vollo.net or https://getbybus.com.

Car tour 1: for the Elaphiti Islands see Walks 1-3 and Picnic 5; for Mljet see Walks 4-6; for Orebić see Walk 7

Car tour 2: for Makarska see Walks 8-11

Car tour 3: for Brač see Walks 12-14

Car tour 4: for Hvar see Walks 15-17

Car tour 5: for Vis see Picnics 14-17

Car tour 6: for Plitvice Lakes see Walk 18; for Paklenica see Walks 19-21

Car tour 7: for Lovran–Učka see Walks 22-25; for Rab see Walks 26-28; for Krk see Walks 29-33

Car tour 8: for Lošinj see Walks 34-36

Car tour 9: for Cres see Walk 37

Picnic 1: see Walk 1

Picnic 2: see Walk 2

Picnics 3, 4: see Walk 3

Picnic 5: Jadrolinija passenger ferry: Dubrovnik–Suđurađ: sailings daily year round, three end Jun to end Sep

Picnic 6: see Walks 4-6

Picnic 7: see Walk 7

Picnics 8, 9: see Walk 8

Picnic 10: see Walk 12

Picnics 11, 12: see Walk 16

Picnic 13: see Walk 15

Picnics 14-17: (1) Jadrolinija car ferry Split–Vis year round, three daily. (2)

Local buses: Vis town–Komiža (daily), also to Podspilje and Milna less frequently. Timetable posted at bus station near the ferry terminal.

Picnic 19: see Walk 18

Picnics 20, 21: see Walk 19

Picnic 23: see Walk 28

Picnic 24: see Walk 32

Picnic 26: see Walk 36

Picnic 27: see Walk 37

Walk 1: passenger ferry from Dubrovnik old town harbour April-November: hourly, May; 20/day June-September; less frequently April, November; www.lokrum.hr/en

Walks 2, 3: Jadrolinija passenger ferry: at least two sailings daily

Walks 4-6: (1) Jadrolinija car ferry Prapratno to Sobra: four daily year round, five daily Jun-Aug. (2) G&V Line (www.gv-line.hr) catamaran Dubrovnik–Sobra, at least two daily year round (but timings Mar-May not suitable for day trips), to Polače one daily 4d/week (3) Kapetan Luka catamaran Dubrovnik–Pomena: daily Apr-Sep; Mon-Wed-Fri Oct; Mon-Thur May

Walk 7: (1) Autotrans buses (www.autotrans.hr): Dubrovnik–Split–Zagreb–Korčula; Vela Luka–Korčula town four daily, Arriva buses (www.arriva.com.hr), Libertas buses (www.libertasdubrovnik.hr): Dubrovnik–Orebić: 1 daily (2) Jadrolinija car ferries: Trpanj– Ploče: at least 4 daily; Split–Vela Luka six sailings daily year round. Local services: Korčula town–Orebić (passenger service) numerous sailings daily (www.gv-lines.hr); Dominiče (Korčula)–Orebić (car ferry) numerous sailings daily.

Walks 8-11: (1) Jadrolinija car ferry Makarska–Sumartin (Brač): at least three daily. (2) Promet buses (www.promet-split.hr; website only in Croatian): several daily Dubrovnik–Makarska; several daily from Split and Zagreb. (3) Autotrans Buses (www.autotrans.hr): daily service Dubrovnik–Makarska; three daily from Split, two daily Zagreb–Split

Walks 8, 9: Promet Buses (www. promet-makarska.hr): Makarska–Baška Voda several daily

Walks 12-14: (1) Jadrolinija car ferry Split–Supetar: numerous sailings daily; Makarska–Sumartin: at least three daily; Jadrolinija catamaran Split–Bol: at least four daily. Split Express catamaran Split airport–Split-Bol: two daily summer only (https://splitexpress.com) (2) Autotrans buses (www.autotrans.hr): Supetar–Bol: several daily

Walks 15-17: (1) Jadrolinija car ferry Split–Stari Grad: at least six sailings daily; catamaran Split–Jelsa at least three daily; Vela Luka (Korčula) –Hvar town–Split (foot passengers only): at least four daily. (2) Kapetan Luka catamarans: twice daily from Split, Brac (Milna), Mljet, Dubrovnik (some seasonal). Split Express catamaran Split airport–Split –Bol–Stari Grad: two daily summer only (https://splitexpress. com) (3) Cažmatrans buses (https:// cazmatrans.hr/en). Catch a bus for 'Sucuraj via Stari Grad' (Friday only) or one on the Hvar town–Stari Grad service: check the timetable as some go direct between the two towns. Jelsa–Stari Grad–Milna–Hvar town: at least four daily; Stari Grad ferry terminal–Hvar–Stari Grad: at least two daily

Walk 18: Croatia Bus (www. croatia bus.hr): Split–Zadar–Zagreb via Plitvice once daily (be sure to board the bus going via Plitvice — a similar service goes via the motorway). Other companies operating services on this route include www.flixbus. com and www.arriva.com.hr

Walks 19-21: Autotrans buses (www. autotrans.hr) three times daily between Zadar and Rijeka pass through Starigrad; Slavonija Bus, (www.slavonija-bus.hr) Starigrad Paklenica–Zadar–Starigrad-Paklenica: three times daily; Starigrad-Paklenica–Zagreb: once a day; Čazmatrans buses (https://cazmatrans. hr) at least once daily between Split and Pula pass through Starigrad-Paklenica

Walks 22-25: Autotrans (www. autotrans.hr) Rijeka–Opatija–Lovran, route 32: several daily

Walks 23 and 25: Autotrolej (www. autotrolej.hr, Croatian only) Lovran–Dobreć–Lovranska Draga, route 36: at least six daily, not all divert to Dobreć

Walk 24: Autotrolej Opatija–Učka (Poklon), route 34: Sundays only departing Opatija 09.40 and 14.00; returning from Poklon at 10.30 and 15.45

Walk 25: *see 23 and 25 above*

Walks 26-28: (1) Jadrolinija car ferry: Lopar (Rab)–Valbiska (Krk): at least twice daily; Rapska Plovidba (www. rapska-plovidba.hr) car ferry Stinica–Mišnjak: numerous daily services. Jadrolinija car ferry Merag (Cres)–Valbiska; Autotrans (www.autotrans. hr): several daily services; Catamaran service Rijeka–Rab at least three daily from March to end Sep. (2) Autotrans buses (www.autotrans.hr) Rijeka–Rab town: twice daily

Walks 26, 28: Autotrans buses (www.autotrans.hr) Rab–Rijeka via Mišnjak twice daily Mon-Sat

Walks 29-33: (1) Jadrolinija car ferry: Lopar–Valbiska (Krk) at least twice daily. Jadrolinija catamarans: Rijeka–Rab: at least three daily. (2) Autotrans buses (www.autotrans. hr) Rijeka–Krk town: several daily; Rijeka–Baška: at least five daily. Foot passengers from Cres need to go through to Omišalj (Krk) or Rijeka then change for Krk town and Baška

Walk 30: add 35min to the departure time from Krk town for departure from Draga Bašćanska

Walks 34-37: (1) Jadrolinija car ferries Valbiska (Krk)–Merag (Cres): several daily; Porozina (Cres)– Brestova (Istria): several daily. Jadrolinija catamaran, several Rijeka–Cres–Mali Lošinj: one daily year round. (2) Autotrans buses (www.autotrans.hr) Rijeka–Veli Lošinj via Malinska (Krk), Cres and Osor: two daily; Rijeka–Opatija–Brestova–Porozina–Cres–Veli Lošinj: two daily

● Index

Geographical entries only are included here; for other entries, see Contents, page 3. A page number in **bold type** indicates a photograph; a page number in *italics* a map. Both may be in addition to a text reference on the same page. Individual entries for the various islands are indexed under the name of the island, but for island tours and walks see Contents.